Surprisingly Down to Earth, and Very Funny

Limmy

Surprisingly Down to Earth, and Very Funny

MY AUTOBIOGRAPHY

MUDLARK

Mudlark
An imprint of HarperCollins*Publishers*
1 London Bridge Street
London SE1 9GF

www.harpercollins.co.uk

First published by Mudlark 2019

3 5 7 9 10 8 6 4 2

© Brian Limond 2019

Brian Limond asserts the moral right to
be identified as the author of this work

A catalogue record of this book is
available from the British Library

ISBN 978-0-00-829466-3

Printed and bound in Great Britain by
CPI Group (UK) Ltd, Croydon, CR0 4YY

MIX
Paper from
responsible sources
FSC C007454

This book is produced from independently certified FSC paper
to ensure responsible forest management.

For more information visit: www.harpercollins.co.uk/green

Dedicated to Lynn and Daniel

Contents

The Primary Years

Earliest Memory

Right, I'll start at the beginning.

I was born on the 20th of October 1974. My mum was Jessie Limond, my dad was Billy Limond and my brother was David Limond. And I'm Brian Limond.

I grew up in a council estate on the south side of Glasgow, called Carnwadric. It was maybe a wee bit rough. Maybe. If there's one thing I don't want to do, it's make out that my childhood was rougher than it was. Carnwadric was alright. It wasn't like growing up in a slum, like one of those old photos of the Gorbals. If you want to see Carnwadric, you can google it. I grew up on Stanalane Street, have a look at that. Not rough at all. And in terms of how it felt living there, it didn't feel as rough as some other places I'd heard of, like Govan or Easterhouse, these places where it sounded like everybody was slashing everybody.

But still, I think it was maybe a wee bit rough. It was just some of the things that happened.

One of my earliest memories of Carnwadric is something I saw when I was maybe six or seven. It isn't my earliest memory, but it's one that stands out.

There was a woman out in the street just outside my house, there on Stanalane Street. She was holding a wee boy's arms behind his back, and she was telling another boy to hit him. The boy that she was holding had done something to her son, so she was giving her son a free hit, in front of everybody.

But I could see that her son didn't want to do it. Instead of taking the opportunity to hook the other boy's jaw, he just gave him a wee hit on his shoulder. Just a wee one. Like a tap.

His mum was like, 'Hit his face!'

Her son gave the boy a wee tap on the face.

But she was like, 'Harder!'

I could see that her son didn't want to do it. He looked more upset than the boy he was hitting. His face was all red and he was teary-eyed. He wasn't upset at the other boy, he wasn't upset about whatever it was that started all this. He was upset because of his mum.

But he gave the boy a slap. A good one. Then the mum let the boy go, and dragged her son away up the road.

That's one of my earliest memories.

A wee bit rough.

But if you want to know what my earliest memory is, it's of me in nursery school, about four, getting to lick the cake mixture off a spoon. All happy.

The Bollywig

When I think back to primary school, I have this memory of me always feeling different. I've always felt a bit different. I've always had this feeling that everybody else knows what they're doing. Back in primary, I had this feeling like I'd missed a day. Not just a normal day where they taught you how to read or write, but where they taught you something else, something more important. Something you should know before any of that.

It's something that I can't put into words. It's just fucking ... something. I didn't really think I'd missed a day, it was just a feeling. But there were times where there really were things that I didn't know and everybody else knew, as if I really had missed a day, when I hadn't. Like, there was a song we used to sing, and everybody seemed to know the words except me.

There was this classroom with a piano in it, and every week or so we were to go along to it, where there would be this teacher that would teach us music.

5

We'd learn a few instruments, and we'd sing a few songs from some songbooks she put out. I didn't like singing; I felt too self-conscious. But I especially didn't like singing the song we always did at the end.

At the end of every class, the teacher would bring out something she called 'The Bollywig'. It was a tennis ball, with cotton wool for hair, and a face on it. I didn't realise at the time, but I think it was a play on the word 'gollywog'. (This was the late 70s.) But other than the name, there was nothing potentially racist about it. She brought out this Bollywig like it was a puppet, and she had a song to go along with it. She sang the song, and everybody was to join in. But I didn't know the words. I don't remember any day where she said, right, here are the words. Yet everybody else seemed to know them. I could make out the words for the first bit, but not the rest. So I'd be singing it like this:

The Bollywig is round and small
It hasn't any hair at all
It lives on hmmm hmmm hmmm hmmm hmmm
And sometimes hmmm hmmm hmmm hmmm
    hmmmmmmm.

At the bit where I'd hum, other people would be singing words. I'd be looking about, and there would be everybody singing. I'd try to work out what they were singing, but I couldn't. One of the bits sounded like 'salted plooms'. Salted plooms? What does that mean? I didn't want to ask, in case I got laughed at or got into trouble for not listening.

It was fucking worrying, because it wasn't just the words to some song, it wasn't just that. The song was the backstory of this Bollywig. The song told you who it was and why we should love it, and the teacher would bring it out at the end like it was the big fucking finale, and everybody was excited to see it. And there was me, not getting it, wondering what the fuck salted plooms were.

It was just one of many instances where I felt like everybody knew something I didn't.

And I never did find out the words. I tried googling it, but there's fuck all. I think the teacher just made it up herself, the words and the tune. It was a catchy wee tune, the sort of thing you'd expect to be a famous nursery rhyme tune, where the words are different depending on where you live. But I didn't hear that tune played again.

But then, about ten years later, when I was 17 or 18, I was in college. And one of the folk in my course starts whistling a tune to himself.

I fucking span towards him.

It was the tune to the fucking Bollywig.

This was a guy I barely knew, I didn't know him from school or anything like that. I just span towards him and went like that, 'Here! What's that you're whistling?'

He said, 'What? Oh, it's just a daft wee song.'

I said, 'Aye, but what?'

He said, 'Just a wee song from school.'

A song from school!

I said, 'Here, it's not the fucking Bollywig, is it?' expecting him to say, 'The bolly what?'

But he said aye, it was! He was all surprised that I knew, and I was surprised that he knew.

I asked him if he went to Carnwadric Primary, but he didn't. He went to some school I'd never heard of, from miles away. The pair of us were laughing. What the fuck was going on here?

I asked him to sing a bit, to double-check that we were talking about the same thing. He started singing, 'The Bollywig is round and small ...'

I was like, 'No fucking way!'

I asked him who taught him the song, and he said it was some music teacher. I asked him what her name was and what she looked like, and it was the same one as mine. The same fucking one. Turns out she went from school to school around Scotland.

We talked about the Bollywig and had a laugh about it. I felt like giving the cunt a cuddle.

Then I said to him, 'Here. What the fuck were the words?' I told him that I always felt pure out of place because I must have been the only person in my school that didn't know the words.

It turns out he didn't know either.

I Blame Carnwadric

I sometimes wonder if I'm a psychopath. Or if I'm warped in some way.

Something bad happens, and I don't really care, or I might even find it entertaining. I don't mean that I sit watching tragedies on the news, laughing my head off, having a wank. It's just that every now and then, somebody will talk about how something is bad or dangerous or tragic, and I'll be wondering why I don't feel the same way.

I blame Carnwadric.

Like, I don't know if this is anything to do with it, but see when I was wee, boys would make crossbows. They'd get a couple of pieces of wood, a hammer, nails and elastic bands, and they'd make themselves a crossbow. They'd put a wooden clothes peg on it, pull it as far back as it would go, and try to hit each other, right in the fucking face. A piece of solid wood, flying at your head at more than 100 mph. None of that eye-friendly foam-bullet Nerf gun shite. Or they'd make ninja stars by sharpening bits of metal, and they'd chuck them at cunts. Or they'd get pre-made weapons, like an air pistol or a Black Widow catapult, and fire them off at people or windows or something else, to see what happened.

And I'd be watching it all, as a wee boy. I wouldn't be horrified, because nobody said I should be horrified.

I'd be watching, hoping that something bad happened.

Boys would put stones on train tracks, to see what happened. To see if the train would come flying off, with everybody in it. When it was sunny, they'd find a piece of broken mirror, head to a busy road, and shine the sun into drivers' eyes. I did it myself once or twice. You're kind of hoping that you'll blind the driver, causing him to crash and die. Well, you're maybe not completely trying to kill somebody, but what else are you doing it for? You don't really think about it. I was only about eight at the time.

Boys would do all sorts of things to hurt people, for a laugh.

In primary school there was a game called Pile On. A boy would get grabbed, and everybody piled on them, like it was rugby or something. You'd be trying to crush them, to see if they'd suffocate, to hear him not being able to breathe – and then you'd stop. Another time, it would be you getting piled on. It was a laugh.

There would be things that weren't a laugh. There was something called the Pole Crusher, that older boys did to younger boys. A boy would be grabbed and lifted up, held horizontally, with his legs spread apart, and rammed into this pole in the playground, so that it crushed his cock and balls. They tried to do it with me once, but I started screaming and crying and they let me go. They got somebody else instead, and I stood and watched, happy it wasn't me.

And then there were things that they'd do to themselves.

They'd do things like make these big rope swings that hung from bridges, and everybody wanted a shot because it went so high that, if you fell off, you were a goner.

Or they'd go to the top of the Kennishead Flats, these high-rise tower blocks, 20-odd storeys up, and they'd sit on the lights that jutted out from the building, because there was a chance you could fall to your death.

Or they'd go up to the tyre factory and steal a tractor tyre, then they'd take it to the top of a hill, one that rolled down into a busy road, then two of them would climb inside and get their mates to push them so they started rolling down towards the road. Just to see what happened.

There was just all this stuff where you were either trying to kill somebody or risk getting killed yourself. And some boys did get killed. You'd hear about somebody falling from the top of the flats, or falling down the lift shaft. It would be shocking news that everybody would talk about for a few days, then they'd go back to carrying on as usual. It was like Russian roulette or something.

It was mental, really. But it didn't feel mental at the time. That's what I'm trying to say. Nobody came along and said, 'Now, now, that's enough of all that.'

Well, there was this Sunday School thing. Some Christian thing, over at the school, that I went to a few times. We played games for a while, then they got out a projector and lectured us about Jesus, to try and make us all good. One day, some boys outside opened the windows to the hall, and threw in a firework. A mini rocket. There was a panic as the rocket lay there with the fuse thing sparkling away. Nobody knew what to do. Then it screeched all over the place, in every direction. Everybody fucking shat it. You didn't know where to go.

It was magic.

I don't know if that's warped me in some way, all of that. It's not that I still go out with a broken piece of a mirror in the summertime, I've grown out of that kind of stuff. But there is still a part of me that's into it. I'm a 44-year-old man with a family, but there's still a part of me that wants to reflect the sun into a driver's eyes, causing him to close them, which causes him to swerve into oncoming traffic and kill about six people, including himself. There's a part of me that finds that funny.

It's terrible, I know. But like I said, I blame Carnwadric. It rubs off on you.

Loner

I might have given you the impression that I had all these pals during my primary school years, and we'd go about causing mayhem. But I was quite a loner when I was wee.

There were people I'd sometimes play with in school or on my street or around the back gardens, where everybody would just be dipping in and out of whatever game was being played. But I didn't really have a best pal, somebody to go on adventures with. I didn't have a wee group of pals that I always hung about with, like in *Stand by Me*, but I'm sure a lot of people were like that. I didn't mind, because I quite liked my own company.

I'd go on adventures. I'd spend summers going for walks, alone, just following my nose. I'd walk for ages. I'd pick blackberries as I'd go. I'd walk to the middle of nowhere, and see some older boys, so I'd hide in a hedge until they went by. Then I'd just stay in there, because it felt good. A wee weirdo.

I'd be alone, but I wouldn't feel that lonely. Well, I'd sometimes feel lonely. I'd feel a bit lonely when I went down to Millport.

Millport's this wee island town off the west coast of Scotland, about an hour's drive west of Glasgow, where my mum and dad would take me during the school holidays. Tons of folk from the west coast would go there, the place would be mobbed, but I'd always be kicking about by myself. I'd go to arcades, play some games, or watch other folk play them. I made pals with some boys there once, a group of boys that already knew each other, who were all staying in the same house. I hung about with them on the beach, playing about for a while, maybe for a day, maybe two. Then one day they had a whisper with each other, and one of them said to me, 'We don't want to play with you any more.'

And I wandered off.

That was horrible, that.

It stuck in my mind so much that for the next few years I'd go back to their front door. Not to chap on it and ask if they'd be my pals, but just to look at it, kind of angry. I'd wonder what I could do to it. Maybe scratch it, or spit on it. Or just fucking stare at it, sending bad vibes into the door, hoping that somehow it would make those boys die.

I spent a lot of those holidays in Millport just watching people from afar, watching other boys and lassies in groups, and wondering how I'd become pals with them. But I'd also not want to be pals with them, in case I got told that they then didn't want to be pals with me any more.

Back home, though, I was happy with my solitary adventures. I fancied going out for some adventures at night, in addition to my daytime ones. My mum and dad wouldn't let me, obviously, so I'd sneak out.

I'd sneak about Carnwadric, trying to not be spotted by the grown-ups. I'd hide from all the folk coming and going from the pubs, I'd hide in gardens and watch them go by, listening to them all drunk and talking shite.

I climbed up a scaffolding once, where somebody was getting their roof done, and watched the folk walking past below. I chucked wee bits and pieces at them, to see them react. They didn't know where it was coming from. Fucking idiots.

One night I went out with a knife that I took from the kitchen. Just a wee one, a few inches long, but a sharp one. I sneaked about the gardens, cutting clothes lines. I felt like a ninja. I felt like a dark force. A shadow. There was a football lying in somebody's garden, and I stabbed it. I went stab, stab, stab, then ran away. Then I sneaked all the way back home, and back to bed.

I liked my own company. I wanted pals, but I grew to like my own company. There was me, and there was all yous. I liked that feeling. I still do.

My Mum, Dad and Brother

I've not said much about my brother and my mum and dad, so here's a bit about what they were like when I was wee. I'll try and keep it short in case you're not interested in that sort of thing.

My brother David is about three years older than me, I think. I can't remember him playing much with me when I was wee, but I remember him telling me stories, making lots of shite up that fascinated me. Like, when we'd get the ferry over to Millport, he'd point down at the foam at the side, caused by the propellers or whatever it was, and he'd say that the foam was caused by sharks biting the water. It'd normally be scary stuff, but it wasn't to scare me. I'd just be slack-jawed, imagining it all. He probably saw that I was into that type of thing.

But he never played with me much. He'd be playing with older boys, and I think I cramped his style. I didn't like his pals, though. One of my earliest memories of David is of his pals being pricks to him.

They did this thing called the Heil Hitler. They held him down on the ground, while another boy stood with his feet at each side of David's head. Then the boy would click his heels like a Nazi, and say, 'Heil Hitler!'

It wasn't dummy fighting. It looked like it hurt, and nobody else got it done to them. They just did it to him. But he still hung about with them. That was the worst thing of all, that these were his pals.

I hated them. I must have only been about five, but I fucking hated them. I remember one of them emailed me when I was in my 20s, when my website Limmy.com was doing the rounds. He emailed to say he liked my stuff, and asked if I remembered him. I said, 'Aye, I remember you were a prick to my brother, mate, right in front of me.' He didn't reply.

I think David then started hanging about with these other pals. Bad boys. I'd want to hang about with him, but he'd always tell me to beat it. He told me years later that it was because him and these bad boys used to get up to trouble, and he didn't want me joining them.

It sounds like he was on a tragic path, but by the time I got to secondary school David had a reputation as somebody you didn't want to fuck with. Which is a happy ending, depending on how you look at it.

Anyway, my mum …

My mum was a volunteer in the Carnwadric Community Flat, which was a kind of citizens' advice bureau. Folk would come round to ask advice about a leak or some other thing wrong with their council house, and my mum would get the council to sort it. Other than that, my mum would spend her time in our house, looking after me and my brother, or watching the telly. She was just like most mums where I lived.

But she had this photo album that I used to look through. She was from Glasgow, a working-class area in Glasgow, but in this photo album she had these pictures of when she used to live in New York, when she was younger. She'd moved there during the 60s when she was 20-something, and I always thought that was amazing. My mum used to live in New York, like on *Cagney & Lacey*.

There were photos of her wearing all these 60s clothes, with skyscrapers in the background, or in an office, or on a train with all these people going to a party. She never looked like a tourist. She was never just standing still in front of a landmark. She always looked like she was doing something, like talking or having a laugh or just getting ready to cross the road. She looked like somebody living their life there.

There was a man that kept appearing in the photies, a guy who looked a bit like Clark Kent. Sometimes the pictures were just of him, doing things like fixing a motor. I asked my mum who he was. She said it was her husband. She'd got married over there to this guy. Then, for whatever reason, the marriage didn't work out, and she moved back to Glasgow about a year later, where she met my dad.

She just looked like anybody's mum, but the photo album and everything else gave me a feeling that I wasn't just talking to my mum. She was this person who'd been places and done things, she had this whole other life before me, she'd even been married to another man before my dad. She wasn't just my mum.

But what you really want to know is, 'Did she give you enough cuddles, Brian? Did your mammy never tell you that she loved you?'

No, she didn't, now that you mention it. I don't remember her ever telling me she loved me or her giving me a kiss or cuddle or any of that. It's not that she neglected me or treated me badly. We'd talk about things and she was funny. We'd watch films together. Her favourite film was *Calamity Jane*, this camp Western musical from the 50s. We watched it over and over. She loved it, and so did I. My dad didn't love it, my brother didn't love it, but me and my mum did. But she never told me that she loved me, and I didn't tell her. I didn't really notice, and I didn't care. But I think I must have, because I tell my son I love him. I tell him all the time. He sometimes says, 'I know, you've told me a million times.' And I'm very glad to hear it. That way he won't grow up wondering if his dad ever loved him.

My dad never told me he loved me.

Thank fuck. Imagine it. Your smelly fucking da telling you he loves you.

My dad was kind of like my mum. He was from some working-class area in Glasgow as well, and he was funny. Him and my mum were always having a laugh, I never heard them have an argument once. And like my mum, he also seemed a bit different to everybody else.

On one hand, he had an ordinary job. He was a joiner, he'd go away for the day and come back smelling of sawdust. But he was also an artist. He went to the Glasgow School of Art when he was younger. He'd do oil paintings and pastels and silhouettes, he'd do portraits and landscapes. We'd have them hanging up in the house, and he'd get asked to do them for other folk. I think that was a bit different for Carnwadric, it was a bit middle class for back then, and my dad wasn't like that. He was a bit of a hard cunt, actually, which makes the artist thing seem so unusual. He wasn't aggressive, but he could handle himself. I saw him in this fight once.

I was coming home from primary school, which was just across the road from my house. As I started walking to my street, I could hear shouting and screaming, and there was my dad outside my house with blood on his face. And there was this hardman cunt, a big angry guy that lived a couple of doors down. He was a debt collector for the local moneylenders, an evil bastard. I stood far away, watching. I don't remember seeing any punches, but I remember this other guy's wife screaming something like 'Hit him with your shoe!' But then the fight was over. The guy had battered my dad.

My dad didn't want to leave it, so he started training. He hung a punchbag up in this lock-up garage that he'd rented, and he'd punch fuck out of it. Then, when the time was right, he squared up to this cunt, and punched fuck out of him. I didn't see it, so I had to ask my dad the other day for the story. He said he was kicking into the guy's face and everything.

When my dad finished telling the story, he said it brought back a lot of happy memories. I was happy to hear it. We hated the cunt.

Barry

Right, things have got a bit dark, with me talking about all these bad things. So let me lighten things up. Here's a cheery one for you.

There was this boy in my class, called Barry. He was one of these pupils that just appeared in your class one day, a few years into primary school. And then, not long after that, he was gone. And I don't know if it was something to do with me.

He appears, this new boy, and right away I didn't like him. I think it was because of his face. He looked hard. There were a few boys in school like that, ones that would punch your jaw for next to nothing. I remember there was a boy called James White, who also appeared in my school for a short while before leaving. When he told me his name, I remembered a song to use for people with names that rhymed with white. I sang this:

James White
Did a shite
In the middle of the night
Saw a ghost
Eating toast
Halfway up the lamppost.

But I got as far as 'James White, did a shite, in the middle …', before he hooked my jaw. We were only seven or eight. He punched me in the fucking jaw. My face felt numb, like I'd been to the dentist.

Well, this Barry looked like one of them. He had a big square jaw, he was pale with freckles, and this straight-as-fuck fringe. My hair's like that when I haven't put any stuff in it to stick it up. When I see myself in the mirror like that, I'm reminded of this cunt.

Anyway, what happened was this.

One day, the class had come in from playtime or lunch, and it was a rainy day. A couple of lassies put their hands up to get the attention of the teacher. The teacher asked what it was, and they said, 'Miss, Barry splashed us.' They were talking about a puddle.

Right away, Barry was like that, 'Miss, Miss, I didn't. They're lying, I didn't!'

It was fucking obvious who was telling the truth.

The teacher went like that, 'Barry, why would they lie?' Then she got out some paper from her desk and gave him lines.

A day or so passed, and we had spare time in the class. Barry was sitting on his desk, near me, reading a magazine. It was a music magazine, like *Look In*. And he asked me, 'What music do you like?'

That was difficult for me. A difficult question to answer.

You see, I wasn't really into music, in a way. It's hard to explain why. I liked music in general, I'd watch *Top of the Pops* and I'd like all that, but I don't think I liked any bands or songs in particular. I'd like novelty songs, like 'Shaddap You Face', or singers with a strange look, like Toyah or Adam Ant, but I was more into how they looked than the songs. I didn't know what most songs meant. A lot of songs were about love, and I didn't really know what that was. Everybody else seemed to know. It was a bit like that feeling I had with the Bollywig. I felt a bit left out, I felt a bit embarrassed about love.

So when Barry asked me what music I liked, I felt exposed. I felt that if I just picked a song, I'd be caught out. If I picked a song with the word 'love' in it, I'd be laughed at, or asked to explain what love is, and who I loved. I didn't actually go through that thought process, but you know what I mean, it was more of a gut feeling.

So I just said, 'I don't really like music.'

He said, 'You don't like music? How can you not like music? That's stupid.'

Then he went back to his magazine.

I felt my cheeks go red. I felt humiliated, even though nobody else heard. I can't remember what I did next, but I can imagine I looked down at my jotter, I looked down at my drawing or whatever, and just sat there, with my pencil on the paper, not moving. My pencil making a hole in the paper.

I hated him. I hated him and his pale skin and freckly face and big stupid jaw. Who did he think he was? Who was he? Who was he to come to my school, my class, this stranger, coming to my school and splashing lassies with puddles, and sit next to me and make me feel stupid? I hated him for saying that.

A day or so later, it was raining again. And we all came back in from lunch.

When the teacher arrived, I put my hand up.

The teacher said, 'What is it, Brian?'

I said, 'Miss, Barry splashed me.'

And then Barry, right on cue, said, 'Miss, Miss, he's lying, he's lying.'

The teacher just went straight for her drawer to pull out some lined A4, and said what I hoped she would say. 'Barry … why would he lie?'

Stitched up like a kipper.

A risky move, considering he looked like he could batter me, but that's how angry I was.

And not long after that, he was gone.

Lassies

As you've maybe been able to tell so far, I wasn't very good with my feelings when I was wee. Well, that was especially true when it came to lassies.

I was down in Millport once, when I was nine, wandering about by myself, and I bumped into a lassie from my class, called Helen. We played about for a bit, even though I never really spoke to her in my class, and she never spoke to me.

Then, one night, when we were in the arcade, she asked me to get off with her. I don't know if you yourself are familiar with the term 'to get off with', but it means to kiss. To snog.

Anyway, I shat it.

It wasn't just because I was shy. There was more to it than that. When I was in primary school, I got mixed up about one or two things. I overheard things and saw things, and I think it fucked with my head.

First of all, I'd see older boys talking about shagging. I must have just been in primary two or three. There

25

would be older boys either in my school or on the street that I stayed, talking about lassies, fannies, poking, shagging, licking out, sluts, cows, whores. I can imagine that most of the boys were virgins, really, but I think it made them feel more grown up if they talked about lassies like that.

Any time I heard about shagging or anything sexual, it was from a boy's perspective, and the sexual thing was something that was done to the lassie. You didnae do it *with* the lassie, you did it *to* the lassie. And then you slagged her off for it.

These boys would do shagging motions, they'd have these scowling faces, they'd make it seem nasty and minging. One of them talked about some lassie's fanny bleeding, either through shagging or poking. They'd say all this minging stuff, right in front of me. Nobody said, 'Here, we better talk about this somewhere else, wee Brian's here.'

All this stuff was going into my head, all this sexual stuff. It sounded abusive. It sounded aggressive. It sounded like you had to be a bad person to do it, you had to not care about the lassie, and then later you'd slag the lassie off, you'd laugh about her. And in some way, the lassies liked it.

It was a horrible way to be confused.

But what's that got to do with Helen asking me to get off with her? Well, I'd somehow got it into my head that 'to get off with' meant to shag.

I didn't even really know what shagging was. It was something to do with putting your willy in their fanny and moving about. And that's what I thought she was wanting me to do, or something like that. It didn't seem out of the ordinary, because I'd heard other boys and lassies my age talk about getting off with each other, so I thought they were all at it. And it fucking horrified me. It was fucking nightmarish.

So I said to her, 'No.'

I remember that I was playing a game in the arcade at the time, and I was trying to ignore her. But she kept asking me. 'Please, Brian. Pleeeease!'

I went from one game to another to get away from her, but she kept following me. I started playing another game, hoping she'd go away. I was petrified. Petrified with a beetroot face. I remember 'Let's Hear It for the Boy' by Deniece Williams was playing, and it made me feel even more petrified. In the song, she was singing about some boy she liked, and here was this Helen following me about.

She put her hands on my waist, and I booted her.

I kicked behind me without looking back. I kicked her leg.

And she went away.

I was fucking shitting it to go back to school. I thought that when I went back she'd be harassing me there as well, or telling everybody that I didn't get off with her, and they'd all laugh at me. Why would I not want to get off with a lassie? What was wrong with me? Did I not know how to do it?

But when I went back, fuck all happened. I saw her about, but she didn't even seem to notice me, like it was no big deal because she did it all the time and she couldn't even remember my face amongst the many. Thank fuck.

As I got older, I realised that to get off with somebody meant to just kiss them. But that feeling still stayed, somehow. That fear. And the feeling that to do something sexual with a lassie, you had to be a cunt. It manifested itself in my teenage years as the phenomenon known as 'fanny fright'. But I'll get round to that later.

My First Computer Program

As a bit of a loner type that was scared of lassies, it goes without saying that I was into computers.

My first computer was the Commodore VIC-20. Before that, we had the Atari 2600, then the Spectrum, but the Atari was more of a console, and the Spectrum was considered to be my brother's. Whereas I thought of the VIC-20 as mine.

After that, I was never without a computer. The VIC-20 was replaced by the Commodore Plus/4, which was replaced by the Commodore 64C, then the

Atari ST. After that came the consoles and the PC. It must have cost my mum and dad a fortune, but that's all I was into. And it's what I've always been into, more than anything. Computers. And I later became a computer programmer, of sorts.

I remember my first computer program. The first program that wasn't just me printing my name all across the screen.

It was done on the VIC-20, when I was eight or nine, and it was adapted from a tutorial in a book that I had. The tutorial taught you how to make a program that presented the user with a series of options that they could select from, with each option giving a different response. When you ran the tutorial, it asked the user what they would like to eat, from a choice of three items. The user would press 1, 2 or 3, and the computer would respond with something like 'Very well, sir' or 'I'm afraid there is no more soup.' It gave me a wee buzz seeing it work. But I had an idea of how to adapt it.

I changed it so that it was a lassie telling me that she liked me, and one of the options was her asking me if I wanted to feel her legs.

I can't remember what the other options were. I can't imagine at that age I put in the option of feeling her boobs or her fanny, but it was something sexual, and I definitely remember the thing about her legs. I think I was into legs because I'd seen the music video for 'Dead Ringer for Love' by Meat Loaf, where Cher was dancing on the bar with these guys feeling her legs. And I wondered what it was like, to feel a woman's legs.

Whatever the options were, when you selected them, I made the virtual lassie reply with something like 'Oooh, feels good' or 'I like that.'

I don't know if it gave me a hard-on at that age, but it turned me on in a way, and I kept looking over my shoulder at my bedroom door in case somebody walked in.

I was ahead of my time.

Proddies and Catholics

I'll say one more thing about lassies, but this time for a different reason. This is something else that was wrong with Carnwadric, and Glasgow in general.

Not far from where I lived, there were these lassies that stayed across the road from my auntie Jean's house. These sisters. I can't remember if there were two or three of them, but one of them looked about the same age as me, which was about eight or nine years old, and one of them was a few years older. I remember being over at my auntie Jean's house, and sometimes seeing these lassies across the road. I'd look at them for quite a while. I didn't like them. It wasn't because of anything they'd done. I hadn't spoken to them. I didn't know anything about them.

The only thing I did know about them was that they were Catholics. And that's why I didn't like them.

I was a Proddy. My mum and dad and brother were Proddies. I went to a non-denominational school, also known as a Proddy school. My uncles were in the Orange Order, and I'd sometimes get taken to the Lodge, or to the Orange Walk. Folk like me were supposed to be into Rangers and the Queen, and Catholics were into Celtic and the Pope. They were into Ireland, and I was supposed to be into the United Kingdom and the Union Jack.

I picked all that up here and there. I picked it up in the house, or from boys on my street, or from watching an Orange Walk going by and listening to what people were saying. I picked it up in school. Our school was on a hill, and down at the bottom of the hill was the Catholic school, St Vincent's Primary. You could see it from the playground, and boys would shout down 'Fuck the Pope' and things like that.

It's not that I lived in a Proddy area. It wasn't like Belfast with the colours of flags painted onto the pavement. Protestants and Catholics all lived side by side and played together. But I sensed that there were these differences to us. I remember starting Carnwadric Primary, and a boy that I played with started in St Vincent's Primary. He came back from school one day and asked me if I was holy. I didn't know what it meant, so I said no. He laughed and said, 'Ahhh, you're not holy. I'm holy.' I didn't like that, I didn't understand it, and he probably didn't either, but I knew it was something to do with him being a Catholic and me being a Proddy.

You were on one side or the other. I don't remember any fights between the sides, but there was other stuff. There were things that were shouted. Things that were spray-painted, like UDA and IRA. There were songs that were sung at night when folk were drunk. And there was the Orange Walk, that would bang their drum louder as they walked by the chapel. I was told that was a good thing, because that lot had it in for us, so we should have it in for them. I didn't know why. All I knew was that I should be suspicious. Suspicious of Catholics, or the Irish. I didn't need to know why, I didn't need to get it. There were a lot of things I didn't get, but you assume there was some reason for it and it'd click into place later.

So I'd look at these lassies across the street from my auntie Jean's. These Catholics. I don't know how I heard they were Catholics, I never heard anything bad about them from my auntie Jean anyway, she married a Catholic. I probably knew they were Catholics because they didn't go to my school.

I'd look at them and try to work out why I didn't like them.

I didn't do it with every Catholic. There were lots of Catholics that I didn't look at. But I maybe looked at these ones because they looked so harmless. They were nice looking, with dark hair and pale skin. But at the same time, they weren't nice looking, because they were Catholics. They had these calm faces, these calm features – it was something to do with the shape of their lips. I wondered if they were Catholic lips. Or Irish lips.

I'd look at them and try to find something to dislike about them, but I couldn't. But I knew that I did dislike them, or that I *should* dislike them, because they were Catholics.

It took me years to get that sort of shite out of my brain.

Fun House

I'll tell you something else that took me years to get out of my head. In fact, I'm not sure that it totally *is* out of my head. It's just a wee thing.

Every year, the shows would come to Carnwadric. You might call the shows 'the funfair', but we called it the shows. I used to go there myself, because it wasn't that far from my house. My mum or dad never went there, not in all the years it came. I'd go myself and bump into folk from my school, play some games and go wandering about.

I once went into this thing called the Fun House, or something like that. It was about the size of a big porta-cabin. You'd go in a door at the front, and inside was like a scary soft play, a wee mini maze in the dark, twists and turns, then you come out the other end.

I went in by myself, and there were these other weans in front of me, making their way through it. Halfway through, there was a wee window that let you see outside. A wee boy in front of me waved out the window, and I looked to see who was there. There were people waving back and smiling.

Then another wean got to the window and waved out. People smiled and waved back, and the wean was all happy. I was happy as well. It looked good.

I got to the window and waved. I smiled and waved.

Nobody waved back.

These people outside who were smiling and waving at two separate weans in front of me, they didn't do it for me. They didn't even smile. In fact, their smile dropped. And I didn't know why.

I got it into my head that there was something about me. Something about how I looked or how I acted or who I was, or just something you couldn't put your finger on. It just felt like people didn't like me, for reasons that were out of my control.

That stuck with me for years. A self-conscious inferiority thing. A feeling that I was a bit of a freak, as well as a strong desire to overcome it. I wouldn't be surprised if it has shaped about half of my personality.

It was only fairly recently that I realised why they didn't wave.

They were the parents of the weans that were waving.

They were smiling and waving at their weans, then they saw me, and they stopped waving and smiling, because they didn't know me. They probably thought my mum and dad were standing behind them and that's who I was waving to.

It's like when I'm waving at my son when he goes into primary school every morning. You see a few weans nearby who are smiling and waving in your direction, but you don't smile and wave back to them, because you're pretty sure they're waving to one of the dozens of other parents around you.

But I sometimes do, though. I do sometimes wave at the other weans. If I'm waving at my son, then he stops waving back and looks away, but then another wean nearby starts waving in my direction, I don't stop waving. Even though my son has looked away, there might be a chance this other wean is waving at me, thinking I was smiling and waving at them. So I keep it going for another few seconds – just in case.

I know, I'm probably overthinking things. Most weans don't give that sort of thing a second thought.

But there will be some that do, the ones like me. And if you're like me, that sort of stuff sticks with you. You end up spending the next few decades doing all sorts of things to get people to smile and wave at you, d'you know what I mean?

The Primary Years, In Summary

So, in summary, I had a few wee issues. I had a good childhood, but something didn't click. I don't know why. What d'you reckon that would be? A learning difficulty? Autism spectrum? Or was it just all in my head?

Whatever it was, it made me feel a bit different. I was alright, really. But then again, I pished the bed right up until primary six or something. So I couldn't have been that alright.

Something just did not fucking click. Something just did not add up. There was something about me and other people that just did not fucking click.

I'll sum it up with this one example.

In the community flat where my mum worked, there was a map of Glasgow, and you could see where we lived, Carnwadric. We were right on the south-west edge of Glasgow. In fact, you could see that the border went right along the road outside the community flat itself, right along Carnwadric Road.

That meant that you could be standing on the pavement on one side of the road, in Glasgow. And then when you crossed to the other pavement, that was you outside Glasgow. You'd be in Thornliebank.

I thought that was brilliant. I thought it was mind-blowing.

I'd tell people about it, other wee boys and lassies, but they didn't seem to be that interested.

I'd ask people if they knew what side the road itself was on. Was the line in Glasgow? The line on the map was a thick line that was the width of the road, so was the line part of Glasgow? Or was it part of Thornliebank? Or did it not belong to anybody?

I'd ask people, but nobody knew, or cared.

I'd ask them if they thought that maybe the border was actually right in the middle of the road, right where the white lines were. Maybe the border was thinner than the white lines themselves. Maybe it was as thin as a wee line you'd draw with a pencil. Or maybe even thinner than that.

Nobody knew. Nobody cared. Nobody ever seemed to care about things like that. It only ever seemed to be me.

Other people seemed kind of stupid to me, the other boys and lassies in my class. Yet I tended to fall behind. I was the last person in my class to learn how to write their name. I'm not dyslexic, that's just the way I was. Whenever we had some work to do for the end of the day, I was one of the last to hand it in. And I was all confused about those other things I mentioned, like music and love and getting off with each other and how to be pals, and the fucking Bollywig.

But seriously, is the Glasgow boundary along Carnwadric Road inside Glasgow or outside? Does it include both pavements, or just one?

You're surely wondering the same thing yourself.

The Secondary Years

My Best Pal

Let's kick off this section with something happy, because I got a bit negative with all the talk about my primary school years. What a downer. I'm meant to be a comedian, an entertainer. So let's kick this section off with something good.

Just before I started secondary school, we moved house. It was only around the corner, really, we were still in Carnwadric, in another council house. We moved from Stanalane Street down to Boydstone Road. And when we moved there, I became pally with this boy who stayed in the next block. And he ended up becoming my best pal.

He was funny as fuck. Full of patter. He was confident, kind of grown up, but always up for a laugh. He was always up for doing all the things I wanted to do, like going on all the adventures I used to go on myself, and I was up for whatever he was up for. We got on really well, considering how different we were.

I lived in my head a bit and he was outgoing, I was a bit stupid when it came to certain social things, and he was full of common sense. But he was bad at reading and writing and general knowledge. He'd read stuff all slowly. He got diagnosed as dyslexic years later as an adult, but back in the 80s he was just thought of as stupid. So there was all this stuff I'd tell him about that he didn't know, and all this stuff he'd tell me about that I didn't know. For example, lassies.

He'd tell me about lassies, and laugh at how much I had fanny fright. He'd say I was 'scared of the baird', baird meaning beard, meaning a woman's beard, meaning her pubes, therefore her fanny. He'd never take the piss out of me in a bad way, but in a pally way. We'd hang about in Carnwadric, and I'd see him with lassies, see him getting off with one, and I'd wonder how he did it, where you started, how you learned.

I hadn't got off with anybody before. I was in second year in secondary school and I still hadn't got off with anybody, whereas everybody else seemed to be doing it.

My mate took me aside one night, and asked me if I knew how to get off with a lassie.

I said aye, but I didn't really.

He laughed and said, 'How then? Go.' He didn't want me to kiss him, he just wanted me to show him what I did with my mouth.

I got embarrassed and said that I fucking knew how to get off with a lassie, fuck off.

But he said, 'Look, you just do this,' then he started to show me, by pretending to get off with this invisible lassie. I wanted to walk away, but instead I watched him, because I wanted to know. He had his mouth open, with his tongue sticking out a bit, and he moved his chin in a circular motion. He said, 'That's all you do. You just move your chin in a circle like that.'

It looked easy. It looked daft, but it looked easy.

Not long after that, he told me that this lassie wanted to get off with me.

It was a fat lassie called Julie that we hung about with. She always hung about with this other lassie that was skinnier than her, and my mate would sometimes sing this song to them: 'Fatty and skinny went tae bed. Fatty rolled over and skinny was dead.' Julie would chase him about for singing it, then batter him. But they'd all still be pals. I think he even got off with her sometimes, her and her mate.

I was terrified, but I said alright.

It was night-time, and she took me round the corner, then got off with me.

I just stood there, doing that thing that my mate told me to do. I just stood there taking no pleasure in it, just getting through it like it was an initiation. Which it was, in a way.

Then we stopped, and walked back. I went to talk to my mate and I told him how excited I was, and he congratulated me.

It was like *Footloose* or something. The funny thing is, d'you remember that lassie Helen that wanted to get off with me in Millport, and that song 'Let's Hear It for the Boy' was playing? That's the song playing in the film *Footloose* when Kevin Bacon's character is teaching his mate how to dance. And there was my mate teaching me how to get off with somebody.

He then wanted to move me on to the next stage of the training course.

Poking.

No, no. I said I didn't want to do all that. I was only in fucking second year, for fuck's sake.

He said it was good. He said you put your finger in the lassie's fanny, and you could walk about later with your finger to your nose, smelling it.

No, no, no. No. That was *Footloose*, except Kevin Bacon's character then offers his mate a pill. 'Take it. Go on, take it. Don't be a shitebag, take it.'

Too much, too soon.

I was happy that I'd got off with somebody and it was over and done with. It bumped up my confidence a bit. Not a lot, but a bit. I went into school, and word got out. It's not that everybody was interested, but, you know, a few folk heard about it. There was a group of lassies, and one of them said, 'I heard you got off with Julie.' Julie wasn't in our school, so I didn't know how this lassie knew Julie's name, but she knew.

I said aye, a wee bit nervous, but a wee bit proud.

Then this lassie impersonated the way I got off with Julie.

It didn't look good.

She pursed her lips tightly, like an arsehole, and squeezed her tongue through it, like the arsehole was doing a shite. Then she moved the tongue up and down, moving the mouth with it. It looked like somebody licking an ice lolly with their mouth closed, if you know what I mean. It looked fucking hideous. And they all laughed.

It was like *Footloose*, except imagine the bit at the end where Kevin Bacon's pal finally does his big dance at the disco and everybody's amazed, but instead of that, imagine everybody points and laughs and goes, 'Hahahaha, check the fucking *state*!'

Bullied

Earlier in the book, you asked me the question, 'Limmy, did your mum give you enough cuddles?'

Now I hear you ask, 'Limmy, were you bullied in school?'

No, I wasn't. Not really.

There were a couple of boys that bullied me for a few weeks whenever I was in art, in first year. They noised me up, slagging off my trampy clothes and my hair. Then they pushed it a bit further. We were making these puppets, making the heads out of papier-mâché, and one of these boys tested to see if it was hard yet by whacking it over my head. It was fucking sore. That's when I snapped and went 'Fuck off!' and pushed one of them away. And they didn't bug me again.

Other than that, I didn't get hassled in school. I certainly didn't get hassled by any older boys, because of my brother.

You remember me saying that my brother got a reputation as somebody that you didn't want to fuck with. I'll tell you what he was like. When I first got to secondary school and the teachers were reading out the names to see who was who, they'd all say, 'Brian … Limond. Limond? Any relation to David Limond? You're his brother? I see. Then we'll have to keep our eyes on you then, won't we?' He was like that. I'd be having to prove to the teachers that I was a good boy. I wanted to do well, I was into my computers and that. It was a wee bit embarrassing to begin with, but the pros outweighed the cons when it came to an older boy having a go.

I was in third or fourth year, by which point David had left school. And I was waiting at the bus stop after school, along with everybody else. There was some older boy that had just joined the school, because he'd been expelled from another. I'd see him in the morning, at the bus stop to go to school. He was a shady wee hard guy that would always wear a grey tartan scarf around his mouth, and I'd wonder who he was.

Anyway, at this bus stop after school, he hooked my jaw. He took a dislike to me, an argument started, then he hooked my jaw. He knew I wasn't hard. He hooked it in front of everybody, and I just left the bus stop and walked home.

I told David about it, I grassed the guy right up. I said he had a grey tartan scarf, and David knew exactly who he was.

The next morning, when I was at the bus stop to go to school, I saw the guy. His face was done in. He didn't look like he needed the hospital or anything, but it was more than a black eye.

He knew I was there, but he didn't say anything. I didn't rub it in. I was a bit embarrassed. But, you know, it was good.

So to answer your question, no, I wasn't bullied in school, not really. I didn't get into fights either. I avoided them. I was a bit of a shitebag, really. There was a hard boy in my class who once offered to fight me, and I just said naw. A few months later, he offered to fight this other boy, the biggest in our year, one of these boys that was more like a man. The man-boy accepted, and the hard boy knocked his two front teeth out.

I was a shitebag, and I'm glad.

My First Wank

As I mentioned, I was a wee bit of a tramp in secondary school, to begin with. My trousers were too short, I had the wrong type of trainers, plus my hair was all flat and shite. I didn't know what to do about it. I wanted to look good, but I didn't want to get slagged off for it. I didn't want anybody to look at me and say, 'Who are you trying to be?'

That's what it felt like. It felt like any attempt to look good would look like I was faking it. It would look like I was trying to be one of the normal boys, the ones that played football and talked about what birds they wanted to pump. And I wasn't normal. I didn't feel it, anyway.

Until I had my first wank.

And it changed everything.

Maybe everybody's first wank was important to them in some way, but I don't think so. To other people, I can imagine it was nothing more than a very good feeling, a new feeling. But to me it was something extra. I think it's to do with the fact I'm circumcised. I'd got it into my head that I couldn't have a wank because I didn't have a foreskin.

Where I grew up, pretty much nobody was circumcised. Nobody was Jewish or Muslim, and nobody was circumcised just for the hell of it, like they do in America. The reason why I was circumcised was because there was something up with my cock. That's what my mum told me when I was older. My foreskin was too tight, or something like that. So I had to get circumcised.

I noticed my cock was different from everybody else's. I'd see the occasional cock on the telly, and it would look different to mine. Or I'd see a wee boy's cock as he was in a paddling pool. Or I'd see my dad's cock. I saw my dad's cock when we went swimming once. He was in the changing room next to mine, and I looked through a wee hole, which happened to be at cock height. And there it was. I don't know why I did it, but there it was, my dad's cock, and it didn't look like mine. It had this big bit of skin covering the end, whereas mine didn't. Mine looked like a mushroom at the end.

I really noticed the difference in secondary school, at gym, when I first had to get my clothes off in front of all these other boys. I had a look at their cocks, and pretty much all of them had foreskins. It makes you feel different, and not in a good way. But nobody pointed it out. You'd think that other boys would point out your difference, but it didn't happen. Maybe because nobody would want to admit that they were looking at your cock.

Anyway, I had it in my head that it meant I couldn't have a wank. I maybe also couldn't cum. I was born with undescended testicles, which I had to get fixed. And I thought that maybe that had fucked things up for me. I was maybe some sort of freak.

You want to be normal.

You want to be doing what all the other boys are doing, or at least have the choice of doing it. I was normal in all the other ways. I got hard-ons, I fancied lassies, I was 'normal' like that. But when it came to wanking and spunking, I had a feeling that it was the end of the line for me.

I was so confused about it all, so ignorant. I remember doing a pish in the school urinal one day. I was in there myself, and I had a hard-on. I was looking at the bubbles caused by the impact of the pish against the water, and I was wondering if the bubbles were spunk. That's how ignorant I was. A confused and naive wee boy, feeling left behind.

But that all changed with this first wank.

My best pal, that one I was telling you about, he had this older sister. I wasn't particularly interested in her, she was about four or five years older than me, practically a grown woman, and she'd pace about his house in denims and a jumper. Nothing that turned my head.

But then, one day, she wore leggings.

And I saw her arse.

A sticky-outy arse.

She had these long legs, these wide hips, and this sticky-outy arse. Like an athlete.

I think my jaw hit the ground. I probably reached for a cushion to cover my hard-on, I imagine.

I thought about her all the time, I'd get hard-ons thinking about her. Thinking about her arse. I'd fantasise about touching her arse, my hand on her arse, squeezing her arse, cuddling her with my hands on her arse.

I'd go over to my pal's, looking forward to seeing her. Sometimes she wasn't wearing leggings, but I'd know that under whatever she was wearing was her arse. Then on other days she'd be wearing her leggings again. Sometimes she'd bend over to pick things up, bend all the way over with her legs straight.

One day she was in the hall, ironing, and I had to squeeze past her, and she had those leggings on. The front of me brushed against her arse. And I think that's what led me to having the wank. That was it.

I stayed over at his, in this wee spare room to myself. Everybody was sleeping, and I was lying there in the dark with my hard-on. I'd hold it and grab it and just think about my pal's sister, think about her arse. I'd think about me squeezing past her, and how she didn't move away to let me past, and I'd wonder if she knew I fancied her. I started imagining different scenarios where she'd say and do things to me, a bit like my first computer program. I imagined her pushing her big arse up against me and not letting me past, with her saying, 'Do you like that?'

I started having a wank.

I don't know if I knew what to do or how long for. I might have picked it up from people talking about it or people doing wanking hand gestures. I probably picked it up from my mate talking about it. Well, here you go, mate.

I started moving it about, then, after a while, it felt like things were going somewhere. It didn't feel like I was just playing with my cock, but that I was doing something. It felt better as I kept on doing it. And all the time I was thinking about my pal's sister, her pushing back against me, grinding her arse into me, her maybe taking me into her room and making me do things to her. Making me do things with her arse.

And then I started getting this feeling. A feeling like maybe my hard-on was getting even harder, even though it was hard already. There was a warm feeling in my face, and in my chest. I started breathing dead fast, like I was hyperventilating.

Then I came.

My cock took on a life of its own, and it started shooting this stuff out that had never come out before. I could feel these spasms, and a liquid hitting my belly and my chest.

I just lay there for a second, not doing anything, not knowing what had happened exactly, not knowing how much of it there was or where it all went. I couldn't see very well in the dark, but I could see some of it on my belly, shining.

I touched it. It didn't feel like pish. It was thick.

Oh my God. Was this …?

I put my fingers to my nose and smelled it, and it smelled like nothing that had come from my body before.

It was spunk!

Well, of course it was, but … I just didn't think that I'd ever …

Oh my God, I'd just spunked!

I'd just had a wank, and I'd just spunked. I can spunk! I can spunk, I can spunk! I can spunk like other guys!

I'm normal!

That was the feeling. That was the big feeling. That was the big moment, the big realisation. I'm *normal*!

I'm a man. I'm a fucking man. I could actually have weans, if I wanted. I'm normal! The circumcision thing, the undescended balls thing, forget all about it now, forget all about it. Because this here, this stuff on my belly here, this is spunk! Hahahahaha!

It honestly changed everything.

I told my mum that my clothes didn't fit me any more, that they were wee boy's clothes, all the other boys had better clothes than me. So she gave me some money and I went straight to Concept Man to get myself an upgrade.

Because I can *spunk*!

Millport: Rebooted

Things just kept on getting better.

When I was about 14, I went back down to Millport with my mum. I don't know why, there was nobody there, and I had pals back in Glasgow. I probably fancied going to the arcades to play some games. In Millport, they didn't chuck you out for being under 18 like they did back home.

I went out for a walk, I turned a corner, and walking towards me was one of my pals from Glasgow. An actual guy I hung about with. That was a first. I couldn't believe my eyes.

I was like, 'No fucking way. What are you doing here?'

He was like, 'What are you doing here? Since when did you come to Millport?'

I asked him the same thing. We stood there astonished. I was delighted to see him. He wasn't one of my best mates, but he was one of the crowd of folk I hung about with.

I asked him what he was up to, and he told me he was on his way to meet up with some folk he knew, and I should come along.

Too fucking right.

I went along, and there was a big squad of people, hanging about. About 20 guys and lassies, having a carry-out, having a laugh. All pals. I got introduced to them all, and they all seemed decent, all welcoming, mostly working class but with a few posher voices, from around Glasgow or Paisley or Greenock or somewhere nearby. It was fucking excellent.

There was a lassie I fancied, and we got chatting. And I got off with her that very night. The next night, the lassie got off with somebody else, and I was disappointed. But then the night after, I got off with somebody else as well.

It felt like the swinging 60s to me.

Then more people came to Millport, and I'd get introduced to them. Then more. More lassies, more guys. And it would be me doing the introducing. I came right out my fucking shell, so I did.

I mean, I'd already come out my shell from primary

school, and I had pals back in Glasgow, but this was different. This wasn't a wee crowd of five or six of us floating about, like back home. In Millport there were dozens of us, and everybody was nice, or funny, or cool, or laid back. Everybody was brand new, everybody was on holiday, everybody was in the mood for a laugh. We'd all be coming out with patter, telling stories, or saying out-of-order stuff, it was fucking magic.

I came down again and again for years, during the summer holidays and every other holiday available. In summer I'd be there for eight weeks or something, and it felt like the sun was shining every day, and it felt like every night was a Saturday.

Tons of fucking pals, tons of decent people, no shady cunts. And tons of lassies. You know how there were boys in school that used to lie about what they got up to on holiday, they'd talk about these lassies they were with, or a girlfriend they had up at their granny's bit? It was like that, except it was actually happening.

It was a brilliant fucking time. I used to look back on it and miss it, how carefree it was. I even made a sketch about it in *Limmy's Show*.

So see all that stuff I was saying about the primary school years, about being alone, and those boys that said, 'We don't want to play with you any more'?

Forget it.

First Drink

It was in Millport that I had my first drink. I was only 14, but that's quite late compared to the other folk that were around me.

When I first met all these people in Millport, I was the only one that didn't drink. I didn't like the state people got in when they were drunk back in Glasgow. They were a mess. They flopped about, they were half asleep, whereas I was hyperactive. I was like a fucking puppy, full of energy and excitement, and I wanted to keep it that way. I'd tell people that I didn't have to have a drink to have a good time. I was full of that patter.

Then, one night, I decided to have one.

There was usually a big crowd of us, but all I remember from this time was that there were just the four of us. There was me, this lassie I knew, her boyfriend, and her cousin, who was this new lassie I'd just met. I was getting off with this lassie, the cousin. She was a nice person, with braces in her teeth. I think she was having a drink, and that's maybe why I decided to have one, because if this nice person is having one, maybe I should have one as well.

I asked them what I should get, because I didn't want to be flopping about, I didn't want to get in that state. So they recommended three cans of Bud. That was my first drink. Three cans of Bud.

I drank them, and I liked them. I liked the taste. They were like cans of shandy you could get in a shop, not too strong.

I waited to feel something.

Then I started to feel it.

This glow.

I started to feel this happiness.

I remember the four of us sitting in the Ritz Cafe, with me smiling from ear to ear, telling them that it was the best feeling I'd ever felt. I honestly couldn't stop smiling. I had this big smile and a sense of well-being. The other three were laughing at how much I was going on about it.

We went back to a house, where we just sat in the living room. Me and the cousin would get off with each other now and then, and the other lassie and her boyfriend would get off with each other on another seat. It's funny how we'd all do that when we were young, get off with folk in the same room as other folk.

I think the cousin left Millport the next day, and it was time for me to head home as well. We didn't swap numbers or addresses or anything, and I didn't see her back in Millport again.

The next time I saw her was in Glasgow, about five years later. I was in George Square. And I was fucking steaming.

I was waiting for the late-night bus on a Saturday night. The place was busy with people trying to get home after being in the pubs and clubs and student unions, and I was by myself, drunk, and probably being all bitter. Then I saw her in the distance. She was with pals, pointing to a bus or taxi, smiling. She looked nice. She looked like a nice person, just like she did before. She was too far away for me to run over and say hello to, but I knew anyway what state I was in. Even in that state, I knew what state I was in. I'd be a slurring, slabbering monster. Remember me? Remember they three cans of Bud? Look at me now. Ta-da!

About five years after that, I was sitting in work with a hangover, the worst hangover of my life. A hangover that lasted the whole week. And it just so happened to be caused by a weekend trip to Millport.

I'd went fucking daft. I was steaming on the Friday, I was drinking all day Saturday, all day Sunday, I had the Monday off work so I drank all day Monday as well. Tequilas, the lot. Wrecked.

I was still drunk when I went in on the Tuesday, happy as Larry, in my golden hour. But by midday I was a mess. I had 'the horrors', as my dad called it. I was sitting in the office toilet, paranoid, thinking everybody was talking about me while I was in there. I had to get out of the toilet in a hurry, because I was starting to get the urge to just stay in there all day.

There was a new guy that had started, over from Belfast. He was about my age, and he was into a drink and going to clubs. He was a chilled-out sort of guy. I could tell he was one of the good guys. And I asked him to accompany me to the pub, because I needed a fucking drink. So he came along, and I told him all about my weekend. He told me I'd be alright.

That night when I got home, I don't know what was happening to my body, but I thought I was going to die. Genuinely. One of my arms went all numb, for no reason. I wasn't lying on it or anything. The eyesight in one of my eyes conked out for a few seconds. My insides were making all these sounds that I hadn't heard before. It was like my body was saying, 'Nope. Fuck this. Bye.'

The next morning, I didn't feel that much better. I was ironing my clothes before work, and I felt a tickly feeling go down the back of my leg. I pulled down my joggies and had a look, and there was a light brown bead of liquid running down from my arse. I'd shat myself, and I didn't even know it.

I went into work, with my scalp crawling and a feeling that I just wanted to vanish. So I asked that Belfast guy if he'd come to the pub with me again. He came along, and made everything alright once again. Like I said, one of the good guys. And he was like that all week until I got better.

It was a nightmare.

And to think it all started with three cans of Bud, because of that nice lassie.

But wait till you hear this.

See that Belfast guy? I looked him up on Facebook recently, to see what he'd been up to. I saw that he'd recently become a dad. I had a wee look through his pictures, and there was him and his wife holding their baby.

When I saw his wife, I nearly fell off my seat.

Because guess who it was.

It was her. That lassie. The cousin.

I kid you fucking not.

Slashing My Wrist

Millport was brilliant, but it was also where I slashed my wrist.

My mum and dad weren't there this time, they reckoned that at 15 I was old enough to look after the place myself. So I invited my pals down from Glasgow. I had an empty! For weeks!

There were about six of us, staying in the caravan and the wee extension bit. It was fucking magic having them down. We'd all get ready and splash on the after-shave, then go and get a carry-out, and drink it with all the folk I knew. My mates were asking who was who, especially who the lassies were.

I wasn't on the pull myself. There was this lassie from

Greenock that I'd met. I really liked her, but she'd went home, and I was lovesick. And what maybe made it worse was that all my mates were pulling. There was all this joy around me involving lassies and guys, and I was in a world of my own, lovesick. Maybe I was jealous, fuck knows, but I think it was something else, something that wasn't even about the lassie or my mates, something going way back.

And what made things worst of all was that I was drunk.

I was drunk, and I wanted to see her. I wanted to speak to her. So I phoned her. I'd phone her and hear her voice and everything would be alright.

I went to a phone box, and gave her a phone. I can't remember much of the conversation, but I remember one thing.

I said to her, 'I love you.'

This was a lassie I hardly knew. I mean, how long had I known her for? A week? A few fucking days? And we hadn't even shagged or anything like that. We got off with each other a few times. We talked, though, we got on. I liked chatting with her, so I just latched on. I latched right on. And I told her I loved her.

I wanted to hear it back. I wanted to hear her say that she loved me as well.

But she just said, 'Right.'

It wasn't what I wanted to hear.

I said, 'Do you love me?'

She said, 'Em … I like you. I don't love you. We haven't known each other for that long.'

I was like, 'But I love you.'

I started crying. My voice went all high. I was like that for the rest of the conversation, with me telling her how much I loved her and how much I wanted to see her. And there she was having to deal with this drunken fucking loony, having to let him down gently.

When we finished chatting I stayed in the phone box for a while, crying. When I left I bumped into my mates, and told them I couldn't take it any more, and I was going to go back to the caravan and get a knife and kill myself. They said I was overreacting, but they followed me back. I went into the kitchen drawer, but I couldn't find a sharp enough knife, so I took a fork.

That's right, a fork. A blunt one at that.

I ran away, with them chasing me. One of them started crying, telling me that he loved me. I said I was sorry, but I needed to do it, I hated my life, I hated myself, I was a fucking joke. I probably spilled out all sorts of reasons why I hated my life, stuff going back to primary school.

I managed to get away from them, but I could hear them shouting for me. I liked it, in a way, but not in the way that put a smile on my face. I liked that I was making them aware of how I was feeling.

When I couldn't hear them any more, when it was all quiet and dark, I just thought about myself. Just bad feelings. Bad feelings. All bad.

I took out the fork, and tried to do my wrist in with it. I pushed it and jabbed it against my wrist, hoping to break the skin, but it was like trying to slash your wrist with a chopstick. It was fucking laughable, really.

But then I found something better, an empty bottle of Merrydown cider. I smashed the bottle against the wall, and slashed my wrist with the broken bottle. I took a few swings at it, but I didn't hit a vein. I couldn't see or feel any blood spurting. But I could see that there was a big, dark gash. I'd slashed my wrist. Veins or not, I'd done it. I'd finally done something about it all.

I couldn't really have wanted to die, though, because instead of having another few goes I walked down to a shelter at the beach, one where I knew people would be coming and going. Nobody was there at the time, so I lay on one of the benches inside and waited.

Eventually, somebody came along, some guy I knew. He didn't see the wrist at first, so he was just asking how tricks were. Then he saw it and started going, 'For fuck's sake!' He shouted on folk, and I was taken to the hospital.

I'd calmed down by that point. I don't think I was numb, I think I was just calm. It was out my system. Whatever I was feeling before, it was gone.

The doctor checked me out. It was just me and him in this wee room. The hospital was this tiny wee place, because Millport's tiny, fuck all happens there. It was this calm white place that smelled of a hospital.

The doctor asked me why I did it, while he stitched me up.

I felt embarrassed. I said, 'I don't know, I've just got … I've just got problems.'

He laughed. He said, 'Problems? What age are you?'

I said, '15.'

He said, '15, haha. Wait until you get to my age. You have a wife, mortgage, children. Then you will have problems.'

Now, you might think that's insensitive. It's maybe something a doctor would get sued for these days. But it actually helped. The way he just laughed it off as he was stitching me up. It was his accent as well, maybe an Indian accent: 'Then you vill have problems.' It was like he'd been through a lot more than me to get to where he was, and if he could do it, I could do it. Or something.

I was told to stay there overnight, which I was happy to do. I woke up the next day in the hospital bed. It was a bright morning, with sunshine pouring through the windows. I was told that my dad would be coming from Glasgow to get me, and I'd be going home that day, so I was just thinking about what I'd say to him and my mum when I saw them. I felt relaxed, though.

Eventually, people started turning up. My mates from Glasgow turned up, and they were smiling and calling me a mad bastard. I said sorry for everything, and they told me not to worry about it. Then they went away and some more people turned up later. That went on for a while. I liked it. It was embarrassing, though, like I felt the need to slash my wrist because I'm special and I'm deserving of special attention. But I did like it. If you're feeling down, I definitely recommend it. No, I'm joking.

My dad and brother turned up, and they were shaking their head, asking what I did a stupid thing like that for. I told them I got drunk and I didnae really know why I did it, I just felt down. We drove back and didnae talk about it, we just talked about other stuff like it hadn't happened. When I got home, my mum was the same way as my dad and brother. The conversation about it must have lasted no more than a minute. My mum and dad weren't into big conversations about feelings, whereas I'm the type of cunt that can go on about them a bit too much. As you've maybe noticed.

I was taken to a counsellor, a one-off meeting where I said I wouldn't do it again, and the counsellor said okay then, and away I went.

As for the lassie from Greenock, I met up with her, in Glasgow. We hung about for a day, just fannying about, chatting. I don't even think I got off with her, it was all quite friendly. Then we didn't meet up again. I can't remember if we decided we were just pals, or if we just didn't bother getting back in touch. Either way, I was fine with it. I had a pretty easy-osey attitude about it all, considering I'd slashed my wrist a month or two beforehand.

Fucking Up School

About halfway through fifth year in school I decided to move from Hillpark Secondary to Shawlands Academy. It was right in the middle of me doing my Highers, and because of that I ended up failing them. Failed the lot of them.

Now, why would I go and do a thing like that? Why would I move school and risk failing my Highers? Was I being battered in Hillpark or something?

No. It was because I was loved up with this lassie from Shawlands Academy, and I wanted to be with her all the time.

This is like the third time I'd fucked things up because of a lassie. This is the final part of the trilogy. First the drinking, then the wrist, then this. It wasn't their fault, obviously, and I would have fucked things up anyway. In fact, this lassie was only part of the reason I moved school.

It was mostly because the people at Shawlands Academy had better clothes.

I'm not joking.

Remember I said that I was a bit of a tramp when I started secondary and that I was mostly interested in doing well and proving myself. Well, it was kind of the opposite by fifth year.

Me and my mates were right into all the designer gear. We were all from council estates, but we'd save up our monthly £30 family allowance and blow it on one John Richmond Destroy T-shirt or a Junior Gaultier top or something else that made us look a bit better than we were. We'd go to the under-18s like Fury Murray's and the Tunnel and Tin Pan Alley and rub shoulders with all these other youngsters from better areas, dripping with money, these 15-year-olds with posh accents and £500 John Richmond jackets. We couldn't keep up, but we did our best to look the part. We'd also do our best to sound the part. If a lassie asked me where I was from, I wouldn't say I was from Carnwadric. I'd say I was from Thornliebank. Things like that.

I started noticing that a lot of these trendy folk went to Shawlands Academy or St Ninians, whereas none of them went to Hillpark. All my mates were Catholics, so they were at St Ninians, making me about the trendiest cunt in Hillpark at the time. I'd sometimes wear some of my gear into school, almost to show off, to make up for feeling like a tramp back when I started. Some folk would have imitations of the designer gear I had, like I'd have Junior Gaultier and they'd have Benzini Junior, and they'd slag me off for having what they believed to be a rip-off. And I'd be like, 'Oh my God, you just don't have a fucking clue, man.' Really making up for my trampy period, really enjoying my superiority.

Anyway, this lassie.

I met her during the summer holidays before fifth year, and we really liked each other. She was into all the gear, she came from a better area with a better house, and she had a posher voice. Plus she went to Shawlands Academy. I felt like I'd pure moved up in the world.

When I started back at Hillpark and I was seeing less of her, I missed her. We'd meet up and she'd tell me what she'd been up to in school. The more I thought about her school, the more it felt like a better scene. It just felt like where I belonged. Fuck Hillpark, man. I'm out of here.

So I managed to move school about halfway through. Fuck knows how I convinced my mum and dad to let me and what my reasons were. I think I just said I was dead unhappy, and they shrugged and made the phone calls.

I met all these new folk, folk that I'd seen in the clubs. It was all fresh and exciting. People were wondering who this new guy was, I felt all interesting. The teachers didn't seem to take a liking to me, though. I think they thought I'd be a problem, having to get me up to speed with their class. And they were right.

I couldn't catch up with what they'd been doing. I felt myself fucking it up, and I started to just let it happen.

Me and that lassie drifted apart, until we broke up. We more than broke up. I went to speak to her one day and she said, 'I'm not talking to you. I know what you said about me.' I didn't know what she was on about, and I still don't.

I started losing interest in all the fancy clothes. I just started wearing plain gear – denims, a band T-shirt, a denim jacket. It felt better.

Then I did my exams, fucking clueless. And during summer I got the results through for the four Highers that I'd taken. Failed the lot.

What a silly boy.

I didn't know what the fuck I was going to do.

Cutting Myself Up

I maybe should have spoken to that counsellor more, that one from when I slashed my wrist, because I started cutting myself up. I'd get a wee bit of glass, or I'd fold an empty can of lager in half so that it was pointy at the sides, and I'd cut up my forearm. Nothing too deep, but I'd cut it enough to hurt and make a mess.

I really can't say why I did it, exactly. It was a mix of things. I had these feelings that I couldn't express. I hated who I was, I was pathetic, I was this incomplete person, something wasn't right with me, everybody else seemed to take things in their stride but it felt harder for me, I wanted to send a message to people, I wanted to send a message to myself, I wanted somebody to help me, I wanted me to help me, but there was no reason for me to get special treatment and I was sorry for everything and I was angry, angry at myself and angry with people and angry with how things were, but it wasn't normal anger, it was something else, it was a sad type of anger. I didn't know what it was.

So I'd cut up my arm.

By doing that, it was like I didn't have to put my feelings into words. I didn't have to write it down in a diary, or write a letter to somebody and somehow find the words for what I was feeling, because fuck knows how I would begin to do that. So I'd cut my arm. It would be sore, and I'd like it. It was a relief. I'd see the cuts and the blood, I'd see this horrible thing I was doing to myself, and it just made sense. That there, that mess I was making of myself, that's how I felt.

I don't know why I was like that, I don't know why I've always been a bit like that. All bottled up. I remember being like that in primary school. I remember this one wee incident in particular.

I was in primary one or two, sitting at my desk, doing a drawing. It was around Christmastime, so we were all doing drawings of Santa and things like that, while the teacher put tinsel up.

I was drawing away, when the teacher walked up to me and put some tinsel around my neck. I didn't know what she was doing to begin with, then I saw what it was. She was smiling, she was a good teacher, maybe my favourite. But I didn't like it.

Everybody turned around and looked at me, and some of them started laughing. They weren't all point-ing and pissing themselves, but they thought it was funny. And my face went bright fucking red. I didn't know what to do.

I pulled at it to get it off, but my teacher had tied it in a double knot. I tried pulling it over my head, but it was too tight. And the class was laughing.

I pulled it really hard against my neck to try and snap it, till it started to hurt. I saw that the teacher looked concerned. So I kept pulling it against my neck to show her I was hurting myself, to show her how much I didn't like it.

I didn't know how to just ask her to take it off, or how to handle any of it. She rushed over and cut it off with scissors, and asked if I was alright. But I just went back to my drawing, embarrassed.

That was like my first instance of self-harm, if you like. Maybe I've always been like that, or maybe the tinsel incident planted a seed, fuck knows.

I remember my last instance. I remember when I stopped.

I stopped because there was this lassie I was going out with for a few weeks in school, a while after breaking up with that lassie I moved school for. One day she asked me back to her house during lunchtime, because it would be empty, and I was scared that she wanted me to shag her or something. I went back with her, though, but we just talked. I didn't even get off with her, just in case it led anywhere. I was scared of being intimate. I just couldn't shake off that feeling from earlier in secondary school, that low self-confidence, and that feeling that went all the way back to primary school where I felt out of my depth. I just couldn't break through that barrier, as much as I wanted to. If I was drunk I could have a go at it, but not when I was sober, no way.

So I started cutting up my hand. I didn't do it there and then or anything, but later in the week. It was partly for self-loathing reasons, but partly because I wanted her to spot it. She did spot it, and asked why I did it. I don't know if I said why. I probably didn't even know myself at the time. It was maybe a way to get some intimacy, through her worrying and talking to me. Maybe she could work everything out.

One night, she said she wanted to show me something. She took off her glove, and she'd cut up her hand. It was all scratched, like mine.

And I just fucking stopped.

My First Acid

I took my first acid when I was 16. It was during that summer after fifth year, when I knew I'd fucked up my exams. I don't know if that had anything to do with me deciding to take it, like I'd 'turned to the drugs', but that's when I took it anyway. It was 1991, and everybody was taking it.

The acid I got wasn't like the acid I saw on the news. It wasn't a square bit of paper with a cartoon on it. It was something called a purple microdot and looked like the head of a match. I was told that it was better, it was stronger, it had more acid, it would knock my fucking block off. And that sounded good to me.

I think it was a Saturday night, and we were just going to get a carry-out and hang about round the back of Arden Primary School, we weren't going to a club or anything. So I got a drink, and took this purple microdot, and waited. I felt like I'd be safe with my mates, because they were the mates I was with when I slashed my wrist, I'd been through all that shite with them. Anyway, I wasn't expecting anything too mental. I was expecting all these funny visuals like my mates said, like seeing Pac-Man, or seeing these trails when I moved my hand. A couple of hours of visuals, something like that.

But what happened was this.

It turned my head inside out.

It turned it inside out, upside down and back to front.

There were the visuals, but that wasn't it. That wasn't the thing. My mates never told me about all this other stuff. They never told me about the thoughts I was going to have.

How can I sum up my thoughts? If you've never taken acid, or if you've taken it but you've never experienced it in the same way as I did, how do I explain it? Here's an example of one thought I had …

My dad is just a guy.

That might mean fuck all to you, reading that. It's obvious that my dad is just a guy. But to me, my dad is my dad. I don't call him 'Billy'. I don't say, 'Billy, what time's it?' It's my fucking da. There's a reason I don't call my dad by his first name, or why I don't talk to him about certain things. There's some reason that I can't explain. There's some invisible barrier, some invisible wall.

What acid did was it took away these walls. All these walls that kept everything in their place.

You know how you get comedians, observational comedians, that ask the audience if they've ever noticed some peculiarity about daily life? It was like that, but with everything. It was like that with the thing about my dad, my mum, people in general, faces, eyes, blinking, hairstyles, the bricks that made up the school, speaking, words, money, pals.

What are pals?

I was thinking all sorts of shite. It was like that thought I had about the Glasgow boundary along Carnwadric Road when I was younger, that sense of wonder, that puzzlement, but constantly, with everything, with everything I saw and thought about, with no thought reaching its conclusion, just one overlapping another.

After a few hours, things started to calm a bit in my mind. I was still tripping, but my mind had simmered down. It was getting late, and a few mates said they were heading home. But I didn't want the night to end.

A couple of them said, well, they were staying out, but they were going to steal a motor.

That was another thing that was big back in 1991, as well as acid. Joyriding. My mates said they did it, but part of me never believed it. It was hard to imagine. So when they asked if I wanted to go, I said aye.

We walked up to this wee cul de sac, it was maybe about 2 or 3 in the morning. All the lights in the houses were off, everybody was sleeping. One of my mates said we should keep an eye on a certain house, because there was an old guy there who was known as a curtain-twitcher. But it looked like he was sleeping as well.

Within a minute, we were in a motor with the engine running using nothing more than a screwdriver and brute force. And we were off.

The mate who was driving could hardly see over the wheel. I think he was 14 at the time, but he could drive like a cunt that had been doing it for 20 years. The other one was in the passenger seat, and I was in the back. We were driving down roads at night, stopping at traffic lights, going on the motorway, in a motor that didn't belong to us.

It would have been a trippy experience by itself, but I was also tripping.

We'd been driving for a while when the sun started to come up. Then they spotted another motor, the same type as the one we were in. One of them got out, pulled out the screwdriver, and then we were away with that as well. A few minutes later, we were driving down a motorway, and I was waving to my other mate who was driving next to us at 70 mph. It was like a game. It was like *Grand Theft Auto*. It just didn't feel real.

We got to this country road, this dirt path that they were familiar with, and we started belting it down, skidding about like it was a rally game. I say that 'we' were belting it down, but I wasn't driving. I couldn't drive. I gave it a shot for a minute, but I nearly crashed, so we swapped back. Then we got to a field and started skidding the motors about and banging them into each other, like they were dodgems. Dodgems that cost thousands of pounds and didn't belong to us and had people's belongings in them.

But at no point did I feel guilty.

At that age I didn't think about how the folk would feel, having their motors stolen. I thought they would just be a bit pissed off. I didn't think about how much it would cost, or the feeling of shock, or the feeling of being violated. I didn't imagine how it would feel to have somebody steal this personal place of yours, like a home away from home, you have your things in it, and now somebody's away with it, and whoever stole it doesn't care how bad you feel. When I was 16 I just didn't care. I didn't think. If I did think anything, I probably thought that it didn't cost much to get these things fixed, there probably wasn't that much hassle afterwards. The pixies would take care of it.

So we just had a good time with these dodgems, until one of them got a bit too done in, so we left it and drove away in the other. We headed back to that country road and started driving down it again.

Then we saw the police.

They were in the distance, in front, coming towards us slowly. So we slowed down. The road was so narrow that we couldn't just do a three-point turn and get away. We had to just pass this police motor and hope that nothing happened.

I was in the front passenger seat as this police motor passed by. We had to squeeze past slowly. I looked at one of the policemen, and they looked at me. I tried to look innocent, even though we were driving down a country road early in the morning in a wrecked-looking motor and the driver looked 14.

When the police were out of sight, we got out the motor. We just left the thing with the engine running, and ran. One of my mates said that if we got caught we should say that it wasn't us in the motor, we're other guys, out for a spot of fishing. It didn't make any sense to me. I said that we should split up, but they said we should stick together. I said no, fuck that, I was going to split, so I went away by myself. I ran over the fields until I got to Stewarton Road, this big road that cut through the fields. And I started walking down that.

After a while I heard a helicopter, and I hoped it wasn't anything to do with me.

After five minutes it was hovering alongside me, hovering over the fields. It was a safe distance away, but it was low enough to make the grass move, and close enough to be loud as fuck. It followed me for about ten minutes like that. I was still tripping, and trying to act natural. I tried not to look at it, then I realised that an innocent person would look at a helicopter following them for ten minutes, so I started looking at it now and again.

A police motor come up to me, and I was told to get in. So I did, pretending to not know what this was all about.

They drove me to the station and started interviewing me. No lawyer. I didn't know how to ask for one, I was only 16, I'd never been in trouble before and I was tripping. They must have known I was tripping. When I was in the motor before, I could see in the mirror that my pupils were massive. Huge black holes with just a tiny rim of blue. I felt off my fucking nut. Not only was I tripping, but I'd been awake for more than 24 hours.

They asked me where I was before they got me, and I said I'd been fishing with some mates. It sounded fucking ridiculous.

They sounded like they believed me, though.

They asked who my mates were, but I told them I didn't want to say.

They asked me why I didn't want to say, if I was only fishing. So I told them the names. The real names, because I didn't want any fake names making me look suspicious. They had nothing to hide, we'd been fishing.

When the police had the names, they switched tactics. They said they could identify me as being in the passenger seat, they had both motors, our fingerprints would be all over them, the game's up. I got my photo taken, my fingerprints taken, and I got driven home.

When I got home, my mum and dad already knew what had happened, because the police had given them a visit. They didn't crack up at me, they just shook their heads and said it was a stupid thing to do. The conversation lasted no more than a minute, a bit like when I slashed my wrist.

I met up with my mates again a few days later to talk about it all. They asked me what happened, and I said that I got caught, but I lied and said the police already knew all their names and addresses. I said it must have been that old guy that grassed them, that curtain-twitcher guy, he must have saw us. They nodded and said aye, that's what it'll be, it'll be that cunt. I shouldn't have said that. My mates weren't violent, but still, I shouldn't have said that.

I eventually got a lawyer. I don't know if I pled guilty, but I was found guilty. Two counts of car theft, two driving without insurance, two driving without a licence, and I think I got done for a bit of hash they found on me as well. Because it was a first offence, I didn't get the jail. I got a fine, a few hundred quid.

The rest of them got lesser punishments, if anything. Because I was the oldest, and the only one who was 16, I got done the most. The prosecution said I was the ringleader, even though I can't drive. Even though I was tripping out my box, I got done as the ringleader. I can't drive, even to this day.

After I got sentenced, my mum told me to stop hanging about with them. It's about the only time she put her foot down. I was happy to go along with it, because I was scared of being found out as a grass. But when I bumped into one of them years later, in my 20s, I confessed. I confessed that I effectively grassed them all up. He laughed and said he knew. They always knew.

Anyway, I just want to apologise. Not to my mates, but to the people whose motors I helped steal. My 16-year-old self couldn't apologise, because he didn't care, but I'll apologise on his behalf.

Strip Search

After summer, I went back to school to redo my Highers. I didn't want to, I wasn't interested any more, but I didn't know what else to do with myself. I eventually dropped out, about a month or so in, but until then I was just hanging about. Hanging about like a ghost.

One day I was at the school gates, on my way out, and this guy I knew pulled up outside in a Mini and asked me what I'm up to. He was kind of a mate that I'd talk to now and then. He was a wee bit of a troublemaker, I think. He looked like a weasel, with this laugh that went like that, 'Na ah ah ah ah!' He was like the Artful Dodger. Or Mickey Pearce from *Only Fools and Horses*.

I told him I was up to fuck all, so he asked me if I wanted a lift. I asked him who the fuck the motor belonged to, because he seemed a bit young. I said I'd just been done for car theft and I can't get in any trouble. But he assured me it was his, so I got in, fuck it.

He showed me this wee container of pills, and he told me they were ecstasy, or 'eccies'. I don't know why he showed me. Maybe it was because I was asking how he could afford the motor, maybe he was dealing.

Anyway, we went for a wee drive about Shawlands, looking out the window, shouting at folk we knew as we passed them. We chatted about what we were up to. We then headed to Shawlands Arcade car park. I don't know why we went there, but maybe it was because I spoke about how I couldn't drive, and he wanted to give me a shot of the motor in a safe place. Shawlands Arcade car park was generally deserted.

So he drove us up there. It wasn't the kind of car park where you had to pay to get in. You just drove into it from the road. It was deserted, as usual, so he starts skidding the motor about, like he's in a film. Flooring it, then doing handbrake turns. There were wee corners that you turn around, wee concrete walls. We turned around one of them, and there were the police.

The police just happened to be there, out their motor, checking something. And there's us, teenagers, skidding around in a Mini.

I thought, 'I'm fucked.'

We got taken out and searched, and they found the pills on my mate. Then they arrested both of us and took us to the station. When we got there we were split up, and I told the officers that I barely knew this cunt. Regardless, they gave me a strip search.

Fucking strip search. I was in school only five minutes ago.

They took me to some room, bigger than a cell, about the size of a wee changing room, and one of the police told me to stand in the middle. There was three of them: one in front of me who was going to be doing the search, and two at the door. I don't know why there had to be two at the door. Maybe one of them was there to learn how to do it. Shadowing.

Then, bit by bit, the one in front of me told me to take off my clothes. He started with my shoes and socks. I took them off, and he picked them up and searched them. Then he said, 'Okay, now take off your jacket,' and searched that. Then, 'Okay, your top.' And I took off that. It was all calm and unemotional, like being in hospital.

I knew that I'd be naked in a minute in front of these three older men. That in itself didn't bother me, because we were in the context of a strip search. What did bother me, though, was that I'd trimmed my pubes, which was uncommon at the time. I did it out of boredom; I trimmed them right down so that I was almost bald, just for the hell of it. It looked kind of stupid, but it didn't matter, because nobody was ever going to see it.

But here I was. And I wondered what they would think.

What made matters worse was that I wasn't wearing any pants. I didn't wear any at the time. That made matters worse because I knew that when my trousers came off they'd be expecting to see pants, but instead they'd see my trimmed pubes. It would be double the surprise, and double the embarrassment.

So when the officer said, 'Okay, your trousers, please,' I felt the need to warn them.

I said, 'I don't have any pants on.'

It was a stupid thing to say during a strip search, I know, but you can understand my thinking.

The guy said, 'That's fine.'

I pulled down my denims and kicked them in front of me. And I stood there naked, trying to act like it was no big deal. And it wasn't, really. I looked at the two policemen at the door. They looked at me like it was no big deal to them either, glancing between me and the clothes and the officer doing the search.

But they must have seen my pubes. Or lack of pubes. And they must have been wondering. They must have been wondering what that was all about. Part of me liked the feeling that they were maybe wondering what I was into.

The officer in front of me then told me to turn around, so I did. Then he told me to bend over, which I assumed was to look between my arse cheeks. I thought he was going to do something like spread them with his hands, but he didn't touch me. He just said, 'Okay, stand up, that's you.' And I put my clothes back on.

It was alright.

I'd just been strip searched for the first time, and it was actually alright. Then I was told I was free to go. So that was a pleasant surprise.

I waited outside for my mate, to see how he was and what was going to happen. But I could see that things had been harder for him. His eyes looked watery. I asked him how it went, and he said he got a cavity search. They put something like a spatula up his arse, to see if he had more eccies up there, and he wasn't happy about it.

But I was happy. I really did feel good. Only half an hour before, I'd walked out of school, aimless, with a feeling of my life going nowhere. Then this had happened. It was exciting. That's how bored I was. Me bent over in a police station with a policeman looking at my arsehole. That was a highlight.

Dealer's House

When I dropped out of school, I didn't really know what to do with myself. Everybody I knew was either still in sixth year, or they'd left school for college or uni or to get a job. Then there were other people, like me, who weren't doing anything. They were up to fuck all. Up to no good. So I hung about with them.

I started hanging about in this dealer's house. A guy from school took me once or twice, and because the dealer let people hang about his flat I just hung about there. They were like my new group of pals. There were stoner types, shady cokehead types, and there were the trippers, like me.

But nobody was as much of a tripper as me. I was like the resident tripper. The court jester. I didn't think I was taking acid that often, but I bumped into somebody years later who used to go to the dealer's flat, and they mentioned something about the amount I used to take. I said, 'What, was I kind of known for taking acid or something?' They looked at me like I was daft, and just said 'Limmy the Tripper'. So that was an aye.

I felt kind of safe there, taking acid. I didn't feel like any harm would come to me. I was 17, almost an adult, but a wee boy compared to the older ones there. I was a wee boy compared to the folk my age as well. Childish.

I was happy with that, though. I could be this childish wee boy taking acid all the time and watching people come and go, and I could entertain them all.

But then things went wrong.

I was spending so much time there that I decided to take my computer over, my beloved Atari ST. I'd play games while people would come and go, and I'd leave it there overnight whenever I headed home. But one day I went back to the dealer's, and the computer wasn't there. Nobody seemed to know what had happened. Or, at least, nobody would tell me. But after asking around, it turned out that one of the shadier visitors had smashed it to pieces. I heard different stories about him stamping on it, or breaking it over his knee, or throwing it up in the air and kicking it in half. He just did it out of badness.

I didn't like the way everybody was keeping their mouth shut. I felt like this daft wee guy that wasn't worth helping out, I wasn't worth the hassle. These cunts weren't my pals. This wasn't some hippy fucking commune. I felt like I'd been naïve as fuck, and I didn't go back.

But one good thing did come from it all. I learned how much I loved being a bit of a performer, due to the whole court jester thing. And I have one good memory of one particular night.

It was late, the wee hours of the morning, and the dealer had gone to bed. But there were a couple of guys in the living room with me, two stoner types that I knew fairly well. They were two of the more decent types of cunts that went there. They were melted into the couch, puffing away. I wasn't puffing, I was tripping, and I was standing about, acting out this big thing for them, while they were pissing themselves laughing.

There was this replica gun lying about, a starter pistol or something, and I was using it to act out all these scenarios. I was doing all these wee one-man sketches, involving this gun. That's all I was doing, but I was doing it for hours. And I mean hours. They kept laughing, so I kept doing it.

I was just making up anything that came into my head. Like, I was pretending I was in the local Co-op, and somebody bumped their trolley into mine, so I blew their brains out. Or an old woman accidentally stepped on the heel of my trainer, causing my trainer to come off, so I kneecapped her. Or a wee schoolboy used a sweary word, so I pulled out his tongue and shot it off. The patter sounds shite when I type it like this, but they liked it.

After that night, any time I bumped into those two guys they would remind me of the patter I was coming out with. They'd quote bits and act out certain bits like it was a sketch show. They'd be doing it months later, years later.

There were bits I couldn't even remember until they mentioned it. I said that I must have been doing it for a while, and they were like, 'Mate, you were doing it till the sun came up.' Any time I bumped into them, they'd mention it. I could be talking about something completely different, like how I'd got myself a job and sorted myself out, but I'd see this smile creep across their faces. Then they'd apologise and say that they were thinking about that bit where I kneecapped the granny.

About 15 years later, when I was 32, I was doing my first Fringe run. I'd went from doing a comedy show in a dealer's living room to doing an actual show on a stage in front of an actual audience, an audience who had bought tickets to see me and everything.

And guess who turned up one day? That's right, those two. Every now and then during the run I'd see somebody from my past, and one day it was those two.

I spotted them right away when I came on stage. It was just a tiny room, this place. It was called The Stand 2, a tiny 50-seater room above the main Stand in Edinburgh. It was smaller than that dealer's living room. It took me right back, doing this show for them. It took me right back to where it all began, you could say, back to when I first realised how much of a funny cunt I could be.

Throughout the show I had a wee look at them, to see how much they were enjoying it.

They didn't laugh once.

More Trouble

I started getting into trouble with the police again. I just went right off the rails. This was still when I was 17. That was the age when I just went right off the rails.

I was steaming one night, and on my way home I kicked in the window of an office. It was a lawyer's or an estate agent's or something. I was a bad-natured cunt at the time, when I got a drink in me. I was pissed off about something but I didn't know what.

It wasn't the main window I kicked in, it was the window on the door. I must have been doing it for a while, because it was long enough for somebody to phone the police. I saw the police motor drive by, so I walked away, but they came and got me. They took me to the station, took my fingerprints, took a picture and put me in a cell. In a way, I was happy just for something to be happening, a bit like when I got the strip search.

After I got put in the cell, I had to stay there till Monday, when I was driven to the district court to plead guilty or not guilty. I was in this waiting room, filled with smoke and all these shady-looking cunts. Cunts with big fucking scars, cunts that looked like they had hard lives. There was a cunt with half his hair missing due to some kind of scalding, wearing a suit. I looked at them and thought that I didn't belong there. These cunts were dealt a shite hand, maybe with dads that knocked fuck out of them. And here I was, with a relatively alright start in life, fucking it up. Throwing it away.

My lawyer turned up. I was charged with something to do with attempting to break in, rather than just vandalism. My lawyer told me to plead not guilty, and the trial was set to about a year later, I think, by which point I was in college and staying out of trouble.

At the trial, the witness got up and explained what she'd seen. She said she'd heard a noise outside her window, and looked out to see a young man across the road, walking by himself, headbutting shop shutters. The man then stopped at a door of one of the commercial premises and began kicking it. That's when she phoned the police.

She was asked if that man was in the courtroom, and she pointed at me. She seemed nervous, the way she pointed. It looked like she'd had to rehearse. Turn, look, point, look away. I looked down, because I could see it was a big deal for her. She'd maybe been dreading this day, wondering what type of person I was, if I was going to stare at her or if I was going to try and remember her face and come looking for her.

A policeman then took the stand and was asked to explain what he saw. He described the window on the door as a single pane of glass from top to bottom, and I'd smashed the window halfway up, near the lock, which indicated an intention to break in. My lawyer showed a picture of the door, which was in fact two panes of glass, top and bottom, and I'd kicked the hole at the bottom, nowhere near the lock.

The case was thrown out, there and then. I was very fucking lucky.

But then I got in more trouble.

About a month away from the time that I kicked in that window, somebody saw me loitering around the premises of another place, and they phoned the police. Nothing was broken or anything like that, but I got charged with something to do with intending to break in. And because I still had that first trial pending, my lawyer said that I should brace myself for getting the jail until the trial, because I appeared to be a menace to society.

I nearly started crying.

But the lawyer said that he'd tell the judge that I was hoping to get into college, and that would maybe sway it. Which it did. My lawyer told me to plead not guilty, and the trial was set to about a year later. And, again, by that time I was in college.

I went to court, but the witness didn't show up. So the trial was postponed another year. By that point I was two years into college, with all the trouble behind me. I remember getting a letter through the door telling me that I'd missed the trial, and because of that there was a warrant out for my arrest or something. I ignored it, hoping it would just go away.

One night, when I was three years into college, I was in George Square, waiting for the late-night bus home. I was drunk, and dying for a pish, so I headed into this building site to do a pish. When I was finished I walked out and went over to the middle of George Square for a seat. But then I saw two police officers, a man and a woman, come up to me.

They asked me what I was doing in that building site. I said I was there for a pish, because there weren't any toilets and I couldn't hold it in. They were alright with that, but they wanted to do a routine check on me. I told them my name, and the male officer walked away over to their police car.

I was waiting for it.

I saw him use his radio thing to do whatever the check was. Then I saw him get all excited. He put down the radio quickly and pointed for the female officer to arrest me.

She put me in handcuffs, and I was like, 'Is that because of the warrant for my arrest?'

I was walked over to the police motor in front of a busy-as-fuck George Square. It felt like half of Glasgow was looking at me, wondering what this shady cunt had been up to. It would have been funny if that nice lassie saw me, that one from Millport, that cousin.

I explained it all to the police on my way to the station, how I went off the rails after leaving school but I've sorted myself out now, I'm in college, I'm due to go from my HND into the third year of a BSc degree. I wasn't trying to talk my way out of it, I was just making conversation, and they were sympathetic, saying that they've got to arrest me and everything, but that's good to hear, well done. Then off to the cells I went until it was time to go to court on the Monday.

I was given into trouble by the judge, who said that if I missed the next trial, then I'd be jailed. So I definitely kept a note of that. But at the next trial it was the witness that failed to show again, and the whole thing was thrown out.

And that was it. No more trouble. No more trouble since. Fucking telly show on the BBC. Writing this book that you're reading right now.

I've been so, so fucking lucky.

I went through a period between school and college where I was drunk and bitter and destructive. It didn't last long, and thankfully I sorted myself out. But I could easily have got jailed. And in the jail, would I have got better or worse? I think there are cunts in jail that went off the rails when they were 17 or thereabouts, just like me, but they didn't get the lucky escape that I did. They didn't get a chance to get back on track, and they're paying for it for the rest of their lives. I'm not saying we should tear down the jails and give these poor murderers a second chance and a well-paid job working in a nursery. I'm not saying that. But you know what I mean.

I think about how close I came, and I feel so, so fucking lucky. So lucky.

The Student Years

Gay

I was about to turn 18, and I felt it was time to straighten myself out. The options were slim for somebody that had failed all their Highers, but I managed to find a college that would take me. I saw that there was an SNC Print Administration & Production Processes course. My mate got a job as a printer, and I thought I could maybe do that course and learn printing and start a T-shirt company, where I'd print stuff like those designer tops I used to wear and make a fortune.

But soon after starting the course I forgot all about ambition and just settled down into enjoying myself.

I fucking loved college.

I loved having something to do, somewhere to go. I loved not having to get a job, I loved getting free money and spending it on going to the student union and having a laugh. I just felt less inclined to go off the rails, now that I had a wee bit of routine and a purpose. I did it for five years. If you want to know what courses, I did that SNC, then an HNC Electronic Publishing, an HND Information & Media Technology, which took me into the third and final year of a BSc Multimedia Technology (an actual degree, regardless of what you might think), then a PgD Systems Analysis (or something). I felt like I was getting somewhere with my life, plus I was having a cracking time. I loved it.

Another thing I loved was getting to discover myself, as wanky as that sounds.

College had all these different types of people into different things. I'd look at the bands on their T-shirts and wonder what they were all about, if it was something I could get into. There was a guy who was into Morrissey, one of these fans that had the hair and clothes like him, even though this was 1992/93. He was good looking, sort of pretty. I kind of fancied him, and I didn't really know what it meant – if I actually fancied him or if it was something else.

I started listening to The Smiths, who I'd never really listened to when they were around. All these songs about being sad and lonely clicked with me. I mean, I had pals, and I was going out having a laugh and taking acid and all that, and I was getting off with lassies. But there was something deep down that had always made me feel a bit apart from everybody, not able to express how I felt, and here were these songs about it. It was comforting to know I wasn't alone.

Then came Suede in early 1993, during that first year of college, with more sexual stuff. The frontman, Brett Anderson, was quite feminine and was maybe bisexual, and I kind of fancied him. I just had all these new feelings. It's not that I grew up in these macho surroundings that didn't allow me to speak about it all; I just wasn't around the sort of people that talked about things like that.

I wondered if I was maybe gay.

Was that why I was so fucked up in the head all these years? Was I in the closet and I didn't know it? Is that the feeling I had bottled up inside? Was that why I liked watching *Calamity Jane* with my mum? Is that why I was stabbing footballs and headbutting shutters? Is that why I had fanny fright all these years?

Because, honestly, I had some amount of fanny fright.

I've not told you how many instances. All these times where a lassie appeared to want to take things further, and I didn't, or couldn't. Here are just three.

During fifth year, I was seeing a lassie from another school. We went back to mine, and we were getting off with each other in bed. She asked me, 'Do you want me to take my bra off?' I said no, you're alright. She then told everybody I couldn't get it up, and I got the nickname 'Mr Soft' for a bit. People would sing the 'Mr Soft' song from the Trebor Softmints advert.

During that same year I went back to a lassie's house after a club, and we both had our underwear off to shag. I couldn't get a hard-on. She touched my cock while it was shrivelled with the cold. Another nickname spread around school – 'Needledick'.

During the first year of college I went back to the house of a lassie I'd been getting off with in Millport. We were in her bed, and she whispered, 'I want to see you naked.' I absolutely shat it. I got off with her for a while longer, then said that I was knackered and I slept on the couch.

I'd always wondered what the fuck was wrong with me. But if I was gay, that would explain it.

I had a girlfriend at the time, a lassie who was at another university, who I first met a year before in Millport. In Millport I'd given her a lick-out, the first I'd ever given. We then bumped into each other again and started going out. We got off with each other here and there, but I never tried anything else, not even another lick-out. I even stopped getting off with her, and we became more like pals.

She introduced me to some pals on her course, and one of them was a gay guy. I'd never really got to know a gay guy before, so I was interested in him, but I also liked him anyway. He had a sick sense of humour, like me.

When there was a group of us, I'd flirt with him. I'd talk about the possibility of me shagging him, or I'd give him sexy looks over my pint glass, and he'd say it was turning him on and all that. I liked it. I liked being sexual in that way, almost in a way that I couldn't be with a lassie. And yet, I didn't want to shag him. Not him, not any guy.

I fancied women. I thought about women. I wanked myself silly over women every single day. I had a big pile of porno mags that I'd bought from the all-night garage. I remember thinking that I was wanking too much, so ripped them up and put them in the bin. Then I ended up getting them out of the bin and sello-taping them together. That's how much I fancied women. Yet I couldn't face doing all the things with them that I wanted to do.

But why? Why not?

I think the reason why I couldn't shag women was because I was straight.

You heard me.

I fancied women, I cared about women, I really cared what they thought about me. I don't give a fuck about guys. I don't give a fuck about what a guy thinks about me. I don't care if I'm in a cubicle next to a guy and he hears me doing a shite. Whereas I'd care if it was a lassie, even one I'm not interested in. Maybe that's sexist, fuck knows.

And there's also that stuff from when I was wee, when I'd hear the boys saying bad things about lassies. It made me feel sorry for lassies, it made me want to protect them. I didn't see them as equals, I saw them as fragile wee things. Fragile wee things with the power to destroy me with a wee comment or a rejection or something like that. There was just all this complicated nonsense in my head, and it's a fucking turn-off.

There were only three lassies in my school years that I got my cock out with and tried to shag. Two of them were known shaggers, and the other one was cheating on her boyfriend. It helped me to know that I was just another shag to these lassies. It was almost like shagging a guy, if you know what I mean. But I still couldn't get a hard-on, perhaps mostly out of stage fright more than fanny fright.

No, I wasn't gay. Whatever was up with me, it wasn't because I was in denial. I'd have to find some other explanation for being fucked up. A gay guy doesn't sello-tape together a ripped-up picture of Jo Guest for a wank, a gay guy doesn't go brick hard at the sight of a fanny. Must be something else.

Eccies

Right, forget about all that, let's talk about eccies.

I took my first eccie when I was 19, on Saturday 20th August 1994, in a club/rave sort of place called Hangar 13. I know the date, because a guy died there that night. It was on the news and you can google it. He died from taking eccies.

The police queued everybody up outside afterwards and got their names and addresses, including mine, then they paid me a visit during the week. They asked me if I took drugs, and I said no. They asked me if I knew any dealers, and I said no. Then they showed me a picture of the guy that died, Andrew Stoddart, and asked me if I recognised him. I said no, and that time it was the truth. The police looked disappointed in me, then they left.

It was all over the papers that week. Andrew Stoddart and the dangers of ecstasy, how young people are dancing with death, how you could die from overheating, but also die from too much water. Or die some other way because of these pills.

The following Saturday, everybody was back in Hangar, and back at it. My first pill had just been a half, but this time I went up to a whole one, and I had an even better night. Other cunts were gubbing two, three, seven pills in a night.

I loved eccies. I'd never enjoyed dancing before, I'd always felt too self-conscious. They say 'dance like nobody's watching', but I didn't want to dance, whether I was being watched or not. But now it felt good to dance, and I actually wanted people to look at me, which was a fantastic new feeling. Before eccies, I used to like taking acid and going to the student unions, just sitting and staring at people, full of wonder – but it had run its course. The weirdness had become boring, and too introverted. Now I was jumping all over the place, and it was magic.

There was one time that wasn't so magic, though. It was a nightmare.

We were in Glasgow, about to leave on the coach for Hangar, which was about an hour's drive away in Ayr. A guy got on, selling pills, a shady-looking, stabber type of guy. I wanted a pill, but he looked the type to rip you off. I didn't have any pills, though, so I asked him for one. Then I said something stupid. I said, 'Are they any good?'

He looked pissed off, but he laughed. It was a bad-natured laugh, though, a mocking laugh, the type where he wasn't smiling in his eyes. He looked to the folk around me, shaking his head, like 'What's this cunt all about?' I said sorry, and got a pill. Then he sold my mates some pills as well, and fucked off.

The coach left for Hangar. After about an hour we arrived, and we all got off. There was a big queue outside. There normally was. A big hour-long queue in the freezing rain. And it was time for me to implement this wee idea I had.

You see, people would normally gub their pills in the queue. I'd done it before, but the problem was I'd sometimes be a mess by the time I got to the front, where the bouncers were. The pills back then made you 'gouchy' to begin with, meaning I'd be flopping about like I was on heroin. Plus the bouncers would ask people to take off their trainers for a search. I'd been keeling over, para as fuck that the bouncers would tell me to fuck off. Everybody was in that state, though. But I was para. I've always been para that I'll be singled out. It was the same reason that I was too scared to smuggle the pills in. I'd be that one cunt that got caught. I'd be that one cunt out of everybody.

So here was my idea.

I've got this ability to hold something in my throat and then bring it back up later. I used to do it with coins. I'd let it slide down my throat a bit, then hold it there by tensing my throat a bit. I'm able to talk while I do it, and open my mouth to show nothing's there. Then I lean over to turn my head upside down, and out the thing comes.

Well, I thought I'd do that with the eccie.

I'd have to cover it with something, though, because I didn't want it to burn my throat, and that would be the same as just taking the pill anyway. But the covering couldn't be cling film, because that wouldn't dissolve in my belly. So I had the idea to put it in a chewing gum. I'd hold that in my throat until I was inside, or just swallow it when I got nearer the front, whatever I felt like.

So there we were, waiting in the queue. I chewed a chewing gum for a while, then I got my eccie out and put it inside. I didn't put it in my throat right away, in case I accidentally swallowed it, so I just held it in my hand. It ended up turning as hard as a rock because of the cold and rain, but that made it easier to hold in my throat when the time came. I put it in my throat and walked right past the bouncers, saying 'Cheers' to them, with them unaware that I'd said 'Cheers' through an eccie in my throat. I felt so sneaky and clever.

When I got inside, my pals said they were gubbing their pills right away, so I just went ahead and swallowed mine.

About an hour passed, and I wasn't feeling anything. Then two.

My mates were bouncing about, and I was getting nothing. They asked me if I was alright, but I said I'd been fucking ripped off. That dealer cunt had ripped me off because I'd pissed him off. He'd given them good ones, but given me a shiter. I tried getting more pills in there, but I couldn't get any. My night was fucking ruined. I was the only cunt in there that wasn't pilled-up, and my mates had a right good laugh about it on the coach back to Glasgow.

I got home, brushed my fucking teeth, took off my fucking clothes and went to fucking bed. It was about 4 in the morning, and I went out like a light.

When I woke up, I woke up in a way that I'd never woken up before. I knew right away that something was strange.

Normally when you wake up, you're half asleep. Your eyes open slowly, and they're maybe all blurry. But my eyes just opened and everything was clear. They didn't pop open with a fright, I don't mean that. I'll tell you what it was like. If you were to close your eyes right now for a second, then open them, wide awake as you are – it was like that.

I didn't move. I didn't move a muscle. I was completely still, lying in my bed, thinking about why I'd woken up like that. Did something wake me up? If I waited a moment, would I hear my mum or dad shout on me for a second time? I waited, but there was nothing.

I was lying in my bed, facing the left, facing the wall. I turned my body to face the right. And what happened next was what I could best describe as paranoid schizophrenia.

As I turned, all these voices filled my head. They were as loud and clear as if they were in the room.

They were the voices of other people, of people I knew, and people I didn't know. There was music, from the night before, like a dozen techno tunes played at once. And these fucking voices. Talking. All talking at once. Laughing. All crystal-clear.

I'm not exaggerating when I say it was crystal-clear. I was fucking terrified. I'd never experienced anything like it, even all the times I took acid. When I took acid, I'd maybe hear a sound, a real sound, and think it sounded like something else. But this was coming from nothing. It was crystal-clear and right in my ears, as real as if I was back at Hangar.

Cunts were laughing. They were laughing at me.

I was lying there, frozen, not knowing what the fuck was going on. And I could hear them laughing at me. They were talking about me. My pals. Everycunt.

That guy from the coach, that dealer.

The dealer.

It was that dealer that did it.

The dealer gave me something. He gave me something and I don't know what it is. It wasn't an eccie, it was something else. I'm never going to recover. And he knows what it's done to me. He knows that this is happening to me, and he's laughing. They're all laughing. They all knew about it. All my pals. They knew about it on the coach back, they know about it now, they're all laughing at me.

That's what was going on in my head.

It was relentless. Crystal-fucking-clear, like I had headphones on.

I thought to myself that I could never leave that room, ever. That's what I thought. How the fuck can I leave my bedroom and see my mum and dad again? How could I go to college? I was a goner. I'd heard a rumour once about this lassie that was in a Flake advert, the one from the 80s or 90s where she's eating a Flake in the bath; the rumour was that the actress took a dodgy pill and she went mental and she's in a loony bin. I thought: that's what's happening to me. That's where I'm going to end up.

I don't know how I managed to begin to calm myself down, but I got the idea to take deep breaths.

My da had these Paul McKenna tapes that I'd listened to in the past, self-hypnosis tapes for relaxation and 'Supreme Self-Confidence'. I think I just happened to take a deep breath and it made me feel slightly better, and I remembered the stuff from the tapes.

I began to breathe slowly and deeply. A big deep breath in, and then a slow breath out. A slow breath in, and a slow breath out.

It worked.

The sounds in my head started to fade away a bit, they faded back to how sounds in my head usually sounded. They sounded imaginary rather than fucking real.

It was too quiet in the room. I wanted a distraction. So I leaned over and stuck on the radio. It was 'Put Yourself in My Place' by Kylie Minogue.

I loved Kylie, and I loved that song. It was so nice. It sounded so nice. It was slow, it was nice, her voice was nice. I couldn't have hoped for a better song. I was like, 'Oh fuck, that's better. That's better.'

I was lying in bed, breathing deeply and listening to Kylie. I was feeling better. And it gave me enough time to wonder what the fuck was going on. And I worked out it was that chewing gum. The chewing gum got hard as fuck in the cold and rain in the queue, making it take ages to digest. The chewing gum eventually let the eccie out while I was sleeping. I came up on the pill in my sleep. That's what it is. It's just a normal pill. It was just a normal pill after all.

You're going to be alright, mate. You're going to be alright.

By about ten minutes later the voices had gone and I was simply eccied. I was simply eccied in my room. I felt good. What a fucking rollercoaster.

I phoned one of my mates to tell him the news, one of my mates who was at Hangar. It was about 7 in the morning, but I had to tell him. He wouldn't believe it.

I gave him a phone and he answered it, knackered. I told him that I didn't get sold a dud after all, it was all because of that chewing gum! I just came up! I'm eccied!

He was like, 'Right. Good, good. It's 7 in the morning,' then we hung up.

I put on some techno. Not very loud, because I didnae want my mum and dad to know I was awake and want to speak to me. But it was loud enough for me to hear.

Then I started dancing.

I started dancing in the room myself at 7 in the morning, eccied, like something out of a sketch show. Dancing like nobody was watching.

When My Mum Died

My mum died when I was 20, when she was 52. It just came right out of the blue.

I should have seen it coming, because she'd been in and out of hospital for a few months; there was something up with her lungs or her kidneys. I didn't pay much attention, I just assumed it was fuck all. My dad asked me to visit her at hospital once, but I couldn't be arsed. She'd be out in a day or two, what's the point in visiting? But I went along anyway. I remember being in her room and being a pain in the arse, playing with the telly or something. She called me a dickhead and said I should just leave. I must have been a right wee fanny.

Eventually, she came home again, and there was another long period of her being fine.

Then, one Friday morning, I came out of my bedroom to the sound of something happening. My dad was telling my mum that he was going to phone an ambulance. I looked at my mum's bedroom and I could see her sitting up in bed with her hand on her chest, making this wheezing sound when she breathed in.

I thought she was at it. I thought she was exaggerating. It looked like somebody pretending to not be able to breathe, like she was acting.

But before I headed out the door, I asked my dad, 'Is everything alright, anything I can do?' It was more out of politeness than concern. He said it was fine and I could just go to college. So I left.

On the bus to college, I saw an ambulance whizzing past in the opposite direction with the siren on and the lights flashing. I thought about how it was for my mum, and how these people on the bus didn't know it, they didn't turn their heads to look. It was just another ambulance.

I thought about it in college, but not much. When I got back, I asked my dad how she was, and he said she wasn't well. Obviously. So I was just like, 'Right,' and I went to my room to play on my computer. That was the Friday, and she was kept in over the weekend.

On Monday morning, as I was ready to walk out the door to go to college, my dad got a phone call. When he got off the phone, he said to me, 'Son, that's the hospital. It's your mum. She's not well.'

He was quiet and serious. I didn't know what he meant exactly. I knew she wasn't well, she'd been in hospital, but this was obviously something worse. But I knew she'd be fine. Maybe a part of me knew she wasn't going to be fine, but I just said, 'Right. Well, I need to go to college.' And he said alright.

I thought about it in college. I was a bit tuned out, not really listening to conversations. Afterwards, I headed over to the student union for a few drinks with folk, but I decided to leave a bit earlier than usual.

When I got home, my dad walked out of the living room and into the hall to see me. He shut the living-room door behind him, but I saw that there were people in there. Something had happened.

My dad was that quiet and serious way he'd been that morning. He said, 'Son. That's, em … it's your mum. Your mum died.'

I just nodded and said, 'Right.'

I think I maybe asked what she died of, and it was something called pulmonary fibrosis.

And I was just like, 'Right, I see.'

I didn't feel any grief or shock. I didn't really feel anything, all I could do was think, but I was thinking of nothing. It was like being hit with a logistical problem, one that freezes your mind for a moment. It was like how you would feel if you were planning some sort of event, and you had a last-minute problem, a big one; you're not panicking, but the problem is so big that you can't think for a few seconds. The cogs are spinning, but nothing is happening. It was like that.

I went into the living room, and there were seven or eight women, a few of them my aunties and one of them my nana (my mum's mum). When she saw me, she went, 'Oh, son!' and gave me a cuddle. And the rest of them were the same. I can't remember what anybody said, including me, but after a few minutes I said, 'Well,

I'm going to go to my room, if that's alright.' They all said that was fine.

I went to my room and just thought about it. I just thought about nothing. Then fell asleep.

I woke up, and for a moment I thought it hadn't happened. Then I realised it had. Cards arrived from neighbours, ones that I'd never spoken to but I'd seen, and I thought that was nice. I spoke to my dad about when the funeral was and all that. I was asked if I wanted to see the body, but I said no, fuck that. That's not how I wanted to remember my mum. My mum was full of life. And she still was, in my head.

At the funeral I was almost upbeat. The church was packed, because my mum knew a lot of people. She did a lot of stuff for folk with the community flat and everything, so I was happy to see that. It was like a celebration of her life, even though people were crying. And when we lowered her into her grave, I didn't feel anything then either, nothing bad. I was just thinking, 'Oh look, it's snowing.' It was January, and I think it was the first day it had snowed that winter.

At the reception afterwards I was all cheery. I was speaking to these old folk that knew my mum, and I was saying to them that there was no reason to be sad because she had a good life, she'd went to America and did all these things and she had a family and she was a laugh. One of these old guys was in tears at what I was saying, and I didn't quite know why.

In the week or two that followed, I just wanted to get on with things, I wanted to get rid of my mum's clothes as quickly as possible in case my dad flipped it and couldn't let go. So I went about collecting stuff to chuck out. My dad didn't object, neither did my brother. If they did want to keep something aside, they never said. For all I know, they did keep something. But I didn't. I don't like the idea of it. What if I kept a necklace of hers or something, then one day I lost it? I'd almost be more upset about losing that than losing my mum. It'd be like losing a memory.

I must sound like a fucking robot to you. But that's just the way I'm wired. I didn't feel sad. I never have felt sad about my mum dying.

The only thing that did make me feel sad was when I was tidying away her stuff and I looked in her purse, and in there was a receipt.

That got to me. I felt like I'd been winded.

It was an old-looking receipt, for who knows what. But she'd kept a hold of it, just in case. But now she was dead. She kept a hold of it, assuming that she might need it one day. It was important, it was worth holding onto. You make these plans, you have these things that you think are important, but they're not.

That got to me. I haven't felt sad about my mum dying, other than that. I don't know if it's the way she raised me or if I've got something up with me, but I haven't felt sad about it all, other than that receipt.

The Shadies on the Bus

I was taking it quite well, my mum dying. It was a bit uncomfortable seeing my mates for the first time since she died, or going into college with everybody knowing what had happened. They'd look at me differently, all serious and quiet, which wasn't what I was used to. I just wanted to have a laugh about it all and carry on as normal. But when I got a drink in me, I started going on about her quite a bit, how much I loved her and how brilliant she was.

One night, I went a bit mental. I don't know if it was anything to do with my mum, or if I just went a bit mental.

I was coming home from the student union, on the bus, and I was drunk. I was upstairs, and it was empty except for me up the front and these two guys down the back. And I didn't like these guys.

I'd seen them about Carnwadric. It was actually one in particular that I'd seen about; he was the main one I had a problem with. The problem was that he looked a bit of a shady, a bit hard, but calm looking. He looked a bit like Al Pacino in *Scarface*, without the scowling.

The problem I had with him was that I liked how he looked. There was something cool about him, something attractive about him. He was a new face about Carnwadric. I didn't know who he was. Who knows, I maybe just fancied him and I wanted him to notice me.

I heard the pair of them laughing about something, and I didn't like it. It was like they were laughing at me.

I turned around and said, 'What's that?', like I was hard.

They were like, 'What?'

I said, 'What you laughing at?'

They didn't know what I was on about, but they laughed at me talking shite.

I started some kind of argument with them, about fuck knows what. But then I said, 'Right, me and yous. The pair of yous. C'mon and we'll get off this bus right now.'

They were like, 'If you want.'

I stood up and went downstairs to get off the bus, and they followed me.

Can you fucking believe that?

We got off at a stop that wasn't far from my house. It was near a graveyard, and I said, 'Right, c'mon in here,' and walked towards the graveyard. They followed.

I didn't know what I thought was going to happen next. I basically just wanted to die. I wanted to get battered fuck out of me or killed, or I just wanted something to happen.

I walked inside the graveyard until we were all a good distance from the front gate. They were a bit behind me.

I saw a bottle near one of the gravestones. I picked it up and smashed it, and said to them, 'C'mon then.'

They walked towards me. I pulled up my T-shirt and said, 'Go! Stab me. Stab me,' and I started cutting my belly with the bottle. I wasn't gouging into it, I was just taking swipes so I was making cuts. I started crying, going, 'Stab me. Go!'

The pair of them stopped walking and said, 'You're off your nut,' then they walked away.

I hung about the graveyard for a bit, crying, then I went home.

I feel like I'm making it up when I tell you this story, because it sounds implausible. Why would two guys get off a bus to fight another guy? Why would they walk calmly over to a graveyard for a fight? I wasn't a challenge, I wasn't a giant. And I wasn't rich. It wasn't like they could mug me. I was just some drunken student, looking for attention, from a guy I sort of hated and sort of fancied.

Well, I got his attention. I got a reaction. You've got to give me that. He played right into my hands.

I wonder if he ever saw me on the telly after that, in *Limmy's Show*. I wonder if he pointed at the telly and said, 'That's that cunt from that bus, that cunt in the graveyard, that one I told you about! The one that slashed himself!'

I wonder if he's reading this book.

If so, hello!
It's me!

Evil Presence

Booze wasn't good for my mind, as you've read.

I liked the good side. I liked how it took away my inhibitions and let me do things that I'd normally be too shy to do, especially when it came to lassies. But I didn't like the dark side of it. I didn't like what came after.

One Friday night I was at the Arches, this club in Glasgow, later in that year that my mum died. And I got off with a lassie there, a lassie I didn't know. A ginger lassie. We arranged to meet the next day, for a drink. Fuck knows how we arranged it, because this was 1995 and I didn't have a mobile. But we arranged to meet in the afternoon at a pub called Whistler's Mother, on Byres Road.

I was hungover. Really hungover. I had the horrors, that terrible psychological type of hangover.

I got to Whistler's Mother, and there she was. She didn't look like how I remembered her, though. And when she talked I realised I couldn't remember her voice, or remember talking to her the night before. It was definitely her, though. It wasn't a case of mistaken identity. But I was pretending to remember her, I was pretending to know her. And that gave me the feeling that I was pretending to be somebody else. I didn't feel like me. It felt like if I was to look in the mirror I wouldn't see me, but somebody else.

It had a *Twilight Zone* feeling to it. And that didn't help with the horrors.

We chatted for a while, but I started to feel not right in the head, because of where we were sitting. She had her back to the wall, and I was sitting opposite, facing this wall. I felt claustrophobic, because I couldn't look around and let my eyes wander to the window or the furniture or a telly or other people. I felt locked in with her and this wall.

What made it worse was that we didn't click. I think she liked me, but I wasn't as interested. She was a warm person, a happy person, but quite a normal person, and I wasn't that normal. I wasn't that interested in what we were talking about. I wasn't even interested in what I was talking about. But I didn't let it show. I just pretended.

That wouldn't have been a big deal usually – people pretend all the time – but there was something about this hangover. Something in my mind came apart. There was some kind of detachment.

When she went to the toilet and I was left with my thoughts, a horrible thought came into my head. It was like another personality in my mind, separate from my main one, and it told me it was going to do something bad to her.

It scared the fuck out of me.

It didn't specify what it was going to do. It didn't say it was going to do something sexual or hit her or kill her. It was less about the specifics and more about the intention. There was a will to do her harm.

I had to force it out my mind, like it wasn't a part of me. I remember saying to it, in my head, 'No! You leave her alone!'

It was like something out of a film. It was like *Psycho*. It was like a killer in a film with schizophrenia, the type of portrayal that would have mental health campaigners outraged at the harmful stereotype. Except this was real.

When she came back, the voice went away.

We chatted a bit more and had a few more drinks, and that made me feel better. Then we headed back to hers, some student accommodation place. When we got there, we turned off the light and started getting off with each other. We took off some of our clothes and got into bed, and we were kissing and doing this slow dry-riding.

But, as usual, I didn't try to shag her. I just stopped what I was doing and pretended to be tired, then I went to sleep. The next morning, we listened to a bit of techno, she did a bit of dancing, then I left.

When I got into college on Monday, I told a pal about it, just the bit about us not shagging. I told him that I had no intention of seeing her again, so I didn't want to 'pump her and dump her'.

But he said, 'Brian, it's not like you're just shagging *her*. She's shagging *you* as well.' Which was a good point. That stuck in my head, that. That was actually quite helpful.

I could have asked him if he also had any helpful advice about feeling an evil presence in your head that intended to hurt somebody, a presence that wasn't just an intrusive thought but rather another personality in your mind as strong as your own, and you had to fight it off.

I didn't, though.

But that thing about you and the lassie shagging each other. That helped.

Losing My Virginity

I finally lost my virginity when I was 22.

I'd been close before. I'd had my floppy, fanny-frighted cock pushing up against fannies, sometimes going in by a centimetre or so. But I'd never put my full erect penis inside a fanny and moved back and forth. I never had a shag, until I was 22.

There was a lassie I met when I was in uni. She was in my course. We started spending time together and showing an interest in each other. I don't know how that happened; maybe we all went out as a group in the student union one night, and we stayed out while everybody else went home.

We were quite different. She was a kind of bookworm type, a bit smart-arsey in a way that I liked. I considered myself to be clever, but she was more knowledgeable, and she'd correct me here and there, taking the piss. We'd talk about people in the course, talk about all sorts of things. We'd talk about our past, she'd open up about these bad things that had happened to her, and we'd talk about that, and I'd talk about my past or my private feelings about things, and we'd talk about that. I told her that I was a virgin, and all these hang-ups I had for years. We'd sit in pubs, getting to know each other, talking about bad things and good things. We'd talk about our evil sides and our vulnerable sides. We were both a bit damaged, I think, in different ways.

Then we got off with each other one night on our way to the train station. It was this passionate thing, because it had all been built up. We were pushing each other into shop shutters and grabbing onto the other one's wrists, me grabbing her and her grabbing me. It was passionate, but also a laugh. We got off with each other a few more times over the next few weeks until we decided that we were officially going out.

Our first chance to shag came when we headed back to the flat of a guy on our course, a gay guy we sometimes hung about with. We went to this club called the Garage one night, and I asked him if we could head back to his, and he said alright. We went back, and he said he'd let us sleep in his room and he'd just kip on the couch in the living room.

As I was talking to him in the bedroom, my girl-friend went to the toilet for a minute. I said to the guy that I wanted to thank him for letting us stay, and I got off with him.

I just went for him.

We got off with each other for five seconds or so, tongues and everything. It was the first time I'd got off with a guy. I'd been wanting to know what it felt like, and it felt strange. It felt strange to have his stubble rubbing against my stubble. When we stopped, he looked a bit surprised. I said thanks, and he went away just as my girlfriend was coming back. (The three of us went out for a drink a week later, and he told her what happened, and we had a wee laugh about it.)

It turned out we couldn't have a shag after all, because I didn't have a johnny, and she wasn't having that. It was good to be in bed in the nude with her, though. I don't think we did much. I think we fell asleep quite quickly. The next morning, she got up and got ready, standing there naked in front of me with the light on. We'd had the light off the night before, so it was the first time I'd seen a naked woman right in front of me with the light on. I wasn't quite ready to expose myself, so I waited until she went to the toilet to get ready.

A week or so later I invited her back to mine. I knew my dad wasn't going to be in, so we could get up to stuff.

She brought along johnnies, and this baby oil type of stuff. I said I loved shiny, oily bodies, like I'd seen in pornos, so she brought some water-based baby-oil stuff that wouldn't burn through the johnnies. We put all this oil over ourselves, with the lights on. I had a hard-on. It was the first time I'd had an exposed hard-on in front of a lassie. It was so liberating to be able to do that, and to find out that the sky didn't fall and the lassie didn't run away laughing or disgusted or something else.

We were wanking each other, then shagging. I didn't realise a fanny felt that good. But we had to stop, because she said my cock was too big. It wasn't too long – my hard-on isn't the longest, I think it's about five and a half inches. But she said it was too wide. It was bad that we had to stop, but a part of me was happy to hear it. For years I'd been wondering if my cock was too wee. I'd been in fear that it was laughably too wee. I told her that I was kind of happy to hear that, and she said congratulations.

So we just wanked each other. We faced each other, kneeling, hands all over, poking, pulling, squeezing. I put my finger up her arse, and she put her finger up mine. She hurt me, and it made us laugh.

Losing my virginity in that way was very special. If it had happened at one of those other times when I was younger, with those other lassies, I wouldn't have complained. But having been so inhibited for so long, and then meeting somebody I cared about and loved and trusted, it meant something. It wasn't just a shag. It was like we were actually making love. By doing this thing with our bodies – bodies that we usually covered up, a body that I was partially ashamed of – we were showing how much we loved each other. And by doing it, we loved each other more.

I had bits of her shite on my finger, and she had bits of mine on hers. It was real love.

Data Entry

Of course, we eventually broke up, about a year later.

I'd failed my postgraduate course thing, the one that she passed, and she continued to do her masters. I sat on my arse and did nothing. I'd been doing some multimedia stuff in college and uni, but I didn't know how to get a job out of it. I sent some CVs out to companies, but I got fuck all back. So I didn't bother.

Me and her stopped shagging, and she moved away down south for some training course with some company, and she never came back. She wrote a letter to say it was best that we just broke up, and I agreed.

I was skint and up to fuck all, and my self-confidence was low, so I applied for a job that didn't ask too much of me. Data entry.

I saw it in the paper, and it looked perfect. I was a fast touch typer, so I knew I'd be good enough. I might not get the job if there were people much faster than me, but I could live with it, because it would be more of a criticism of my fingers than of me as a person. That's the sort of fragile way I was at the time.

They got back to me and told me there would be an interview and typing test thing, which was fine by me. I got the train there, to some office building a few miles out. I had a suit on. I think it was the one I wore at my mum's funeral.

When I got in, there were about twenty other applicants, waiting in a wee room. After a few minutes a woman came in and introduced herself as the person who would be interviewing us all. And she told us a bit about what the job would entail.

She said they did data entry for criminal records.

My heart sank.

I didn't have any specific reason for feeling that way, but I just knew it couldn't be a good thing. Just the mention of criminal records, in a job interview scenario, when you yourself have a criminal record. It wasn't a good feeling.

She said that we'd be converting criminal record details from paper to digital. We'd be reading scans of paper documents on our monitors, and typing them into forms. The offices in Scotland did the records for down south, and the ones down south did the records for up here, so that it was less likely for anybody to see confidential information about somebody they knew.

That made me feel a bit better. You wouldn't want your criminal record popping up on a colleague's screen. You wouldn't want the details of all this fucking mad shite you've done popping up, with people talking about you, as you're wearing a suit and working hard to pretend that you're normal.

But then she said, 'Now. Due to the sensitive nature of the information, it means that we won't be able to employ anyone who has a criminal record.'

Oh dear.

She said to everybody, 'So, if that is the case, I do apologise, but I thought I'd mention that now, so that you don't have to do the test.' Then she said, 'Does that apply to anyone here?'

What a thing to ask.

The room was quiet. About twenty of us in that room. Was I to stand up, walk to the door, open it and close it behind me? What a walk of shame that would be.

I sat there and said nothing. I even glanced around,

to see if there were any criminals. Any horrible criminals. Oh, we don't like *them*.

She said, 'Good. Okay then, I'll take you through for the test.'

We went through to another room with desks and computers, and we all sat down. She told us what to do, and gave us something like 20 minutes to type in some sample criminal records. I typed away, doing my best, all the while knowing that I wasn't getting the job. There was no sneaky way of standing up and pretending to go to the toilet and just walking out the door, or fucking climbing out the toilet window. I just got on with it.

When the test was finished, she began calling people through for an interview in her office, one by one. I was hoping I was one of the first, so I could get out of there, but I ended up being one of the last. Each interview lasted about five minutes, so with about twenty people there I was waiting well over an hour. Sitting there. Wondering what I was going to say.

Eventually, she called me in, said hello, asked me to sit down and had a look at her screen to see how I did with my test.

She said, 'Let me see. Here it is. Well, you did great. Very fast. That's great, that's great. So, the job would start ... I mean, we still have to look at all the applicants, but you're one of the fastest, so nothing to worry about there. The job would start around the ...'

I just nodded, waiting for her to finish.

Then I said, 'That's brilliant. But, em, I wouldn't be able to take the job, because of, you know, what you said earlier about the thingy, the criminal record thing. I've got a criminal, em, record.'

She said, 'Oh right. Sorry to hear that. Well, you know, if it's just something minor, if it's just a speeding offence or something. No, in fact, I don't think we could even take you with that, actually.'

I said, 'No, it's a bit more than that.'

'Oh.'

I didn't know what she was thinking I had done, but I didn't want her thinking I was a sex offender or something. So I said, 'It was car theft. When I was younger. I kind of went off the rails a bit.'

She said, 'Oh right. Oh well. No, obviously we couldn't take you on with that, sorry. Sorry about that, sorry to keep you waiting! Oh, you should have said.'

I said, 'No, no, it would have been a bit embarrassing, hahaha.'

'Yeah, haha.'

And I left.

I couldn't even get a job as a typist. Fair enough, it was a job typing sensitive stuff, but who else would employ a criminal, given the chance? Is that really the sort of person you want locking up the office at night?

I just thought to myself, 'You've fucked it, mate. You've absolutely fucked it.'

Flatmate

It was around that time, when I was 23, that I moved in with my mate. He was the gay one that I told you about, the one I used to flirt with, but we were over all that now. I moved in because I mentioned to him that I wasn't getting on with my brother, who had moved back in to my dad's house with us. So my pal suggested I could move in with him. There was a room free, now that his other mate had moved out.

It sounded like a brilliant idea. It was all paid for with housing benefit – that's how my mate paid the rent. He just signed on and did nothing all day, just like me. We could have parties and get people over. And I'd just like being closer to one of my best mates. I'd go as far as to say I loved him. We'd hung about on a daily basis for years, we'd talked about all sorts of things, in person and over the phone. We actually used to chat on the phone back in those days.

There was just one thing.

I asked him if he still smoked, because I hated smoke. And he said he was in the process of stopping. He'd cut right down, and he was about to cut it out entirely. I said alright then, and moved in.

The flat was a bit of a tip. My room smelled of dampness, and it even had some sort of mushroom growing out of a vent behind the bed. But I didn't care. It was my own flat. Me and my mate just sat about all day watching the telly, chatting. We had cable telly, which I didn't have back at my dad's. It only cost a tenner a month or something. I'd watch *The Simpsons*, *VH1*, *Star Trek: Voyager*, all sorts. Mind you, we had to watch it on my mate's black and white telly, because that's all we had. But you got used to it. It was a fucking lovely lifestyle.

The only downside was that my mate was still smoking.

We'd be watching some programme on the telly, and he'd light up. The living room would fill with his stinking smoke from this roll-up tobacco he got from Lidl. It got in your eyes and made your clothes minging. And see in that flat, all we had to wash our clothes was this ancient twin-tub thing, meaning it took about 24 hours to get your clothes washed and dried. But within a minute of him lighting up you were back to square one.

I wasn't too bothered at the start, though, because we were still in our honeymoon period. And anyway, he wouldn't be smoking for long. He said he was stopping.

But he never did.

I'd be getting up to open the living-room window, to let out the smoke. But then it got freezing. So he'd get up after his fag and close the window. But then he'd light up another, without opening it. So I'd have to get up. Over and over like that.

He got up to close the window once, and I said, 'Listen, any chance you could just leave it open to let the smoke out?'

He laughed and said, 'But it's freezing!'

I said, 'I know, but it's the smoke. Listen, you said you were gonnae stop smoking, but you're smoking all the time.'

He said, 'I cannae stop. I'm a smoker.' Then he laughed again.

That laugh went right fucking through me. He knew I'd moved in on the basis of him stopping smoking, and he just laughed it off. I sat there, quietly fucking raging.

We kept that up for weeks, the window thing, until we were barely speaking to each other. We'd maybe say something about whatever was on the telly, so we didn't feel like we'd completely fallen out, but it was horrible.

One day we were in the living room and he was rolling up the next fag, and I said to him, 'Here, any chance you could just smoke it in your room?' His bedroom was connected directly to the living room, unlike most rooms where they're connected to the hall. I asked him if he could just nip in, have his fag, nip out.

He said alright, and started doing it, thank fuck. It was much better.

He did that for about a week or two. He was hardly out of his room, that's how much he was smoking. It was constant. Then one day he said, 'Em … If I'm having to go to my room all the time, I'm gonnae want my telly. I'm not getting to watch the telly.'

I said, 'Fine, on you go.'

He unplugged his telly and took it into his room, and shut the door. And I was left there staring at the wall. There was nothing I could say, really. If he'd taken the cable from the cable telly through, then I would have had something to say about paying for it, but he didn't. It was just terrestrial.

And that was basically the end of our friendship.

He spent all his days in there, and I spent all my days in my room. I had a computer, so I'd play about on that. But this was before broadband. There was nothing to watch. No smartphones. I'd sleep all day and all night.

I did have other people in my life, though. At the start of me moving in, I was still going out with my girlfriend, the one I lost my virginity to, and I had mates that I'd sometimes meet up with. And I'd moan like fuck to them about the situation and how much I hated this cunt. I became obsessed. All I did was stay in the flat, day in, day out, just like him. I'd hear the telly in his room, I'd hear him laughing at whatever he was watching and whistling along to music stuff. Oh, I hated the cunt.

But then something good happened!

I was over at one of my mates', and I saw that he had this wee portable telly that he never used. It was this wee thing that looked like a case for glasses, and when you opened it up there was a wee screen and speakers inside. It was a tiny wee screen, about two inches wide. But it was a colour screen!

I looked at the inputs for it, and there were video and audio inputs. I thought about the outputs for the cable telly box, and the cables that I had, and I thought, 'Fucking yes. Yes!'

My mate said I could have it, and I couldn't wait to get back to the flat. I wired it all up in the living room, and it fucking worked! I had myself a wee colour telly, with cable telly on it. Fucking yes!

I put it on top of the fireplace, which was quite low, just a bit higher than eye level when I was sitting, and I sat right up in front of it, within touching distance. You had to get that close to be able to see the thing.

I heard my flatmate's bedroom door open behind me, and I could see his reflection on the screen. I could see him walking by and looking at this colour telly, with cable fucking telly on it. He didn't say anything. We weren't talking by that point; he just kept on walking to the kitchen to make his dinner. Then he walked back and forth to his room to get things, glancing at the telly as he went by.

Ha fucking ha, you cunt.

I wondered where he was going to eat his dinner, when it was made. He usually ate it in his room, but he used to eat it in the living room, before he took his telly away. So what would he choose this time? His own black and white terrestrial shiter, or my cable telly in full and glorious colour? I thought to myself, 'Please sit down in here. Please sit down in here with it, and attempt to watch my telly. Please.'

And he fucking did.

He came back from the kitchen with his plate, and sat down on the couch behind me. I think *The Simpsons* was on, and I knew he liked *The Simpsons*.

I could see him in the reflection of the screen, where he was sitting. So what I did was I moved my head, to block his view.

Keep in mind that the screen was two inches wide. I just had to move a bit, and he saw nothing.

It was fucking wonderful.

I saw him move over a bit, to try and see around me. But I moved again, so he couldn't see. Then I laughed, at *The Simpsons*. I laughed more than I usually would. I laughed, and we both knew I was actually laughing at him.

He stood up and went to his room.

That's right, you fuck off.

You fuck off into your stinking fucking minging roll-up tobacco room with your pishy black and white telly to watch whatever shite is on ITV at 6 p.m., hahaha. Fuck off!

And then I eventually moved out.

We bumped into each other once or twice over the following few years, and each time there was growling and snide remarks. We fucking hated each other. It was more than just the telly thing. There were other things. That was just one of many examples.

One of the last times I saw him was when I bumped into him about five years after moving out, and a good while after the last snide encounter. I was in a pub after work, and he came up to me to say hello. I didn't expect that, and I didn't expect to see him wearing a suit.

He said he saw me come in. He said, 'When I saw you, I thought sssssss (he made a snake sound), but then I thought, och, grow up, go and say hello.'

It was very good to hear, and we shook hands. And then we talked about what we'd been up to and all that.

Then I mentioned the bad old days.

I said, 'Christ, that was pretty bad how things ended up, wasn't it?'

He said, 'Aye. I hated you.' Then he said all matter of factly, 'I wanted you to die.'

I said to him, 'I wanted you to die as well.'

There was a faint look of surprise on his face, like he always regarded himself as the goodie and me as the baddie.

But before we got into all that again, we finished up the conversation and said bye, with a friendly handshake, and that was it. It looked like that really was it, in terms of leaving it in the past.

Then I saw him one final time.

About a month later I was cycling home from the office. I was cycling through the toon, and as I was turning one corner I happened to see my old mate, my old flatmate. He was standing at the traffic lights, waiting to cross.

He saw me. And he saw that I saw him. But I wasn't close enough to him yet to say hello.

As I passed him, I gave him a nod and said, 'Alright?'

And you know what he did?

He just looked away.

How's that for a twist ending?

Sunflowers

That was almost a year I spent in that flat, doing nothing but going mental. Those truly were the Dee Dee years. Half of the Dee Dee sketches from *Limmy's Show* came from the shite that was in my head at that time. I wasn't smoking anything, I wasn't drinking much, all I was doing was doing nothing. Sleeping, waking up, thinking, wondering, sleeping, doing nothing.

In the room I was staying, there was a poster above the door, a big poster of sunflowers. It wasn't the painting by Van Gogh, it was a photo of two sunflowers in a field, and the two flower heads faced the camera. They were like two big eyes that filled the size of the poster.

One day, I looked at the poster, like I'd looked at it plenty of times before. But on this occasion something bad happened with my mind.

I suddenly became aware of an evil presence, in the sunflowers. It wasn't like the evil presence I felt with that lassie; it didn't speak to me in my mind. This time it was in the sunflowers. It only lasted a second, but it was a feeling that this poster was somehow evil, and alive. It wasn't a hallucination. I didn't see the flowers moving in the wind, nothing like that. I just felt that this thing here, this printed poster of sunflowers, was aware of me. That was a terrifying feeling. It was aware of me.

I don't know if it was because they looked like eyes, I don't think so. I think it was because the picture was just of these two sunflowers, side by side, looking at the camera. It wasn't a picture of a single flower, or a field of them, or a vase holding a bunch of them. It was just these two, side by side. It didn't look like something you'd take a picture of. It suddenly looked creepy, and

I don't know why. Maybe it was the symmetry, maybe they were like eyes, or maybe they just looked like the symmetry of most living things. Two eyes, two ears, two arms. It's like my brain just thought of it as a living thing for a moment.

It scared the life out of me.

The fear of the poster only lasted for a second, but it was the aftermath that scared me more. It was the worry that I had even thought such a thought in the first place. It bounced about in my head like an echo.

I felt like I was going mad. Like, this was it.

This wasn't an eccie in a chewing gum. This wasn't a hangover. I hadn't just woke up or anything. This was simply me going mad.

I can't get across to you using words alone how scared I was. I'd always wondered if I was schizophrenic, if my mind was going to fracture and turn against itself, and here it was. I heard that it really kicked in when you got to your 20s, and here I was.

But then it passed.

I looked at the poster a few times for the next few minutes, to see if I would feel that fear again, to see if it would happen every time I saw the thing. But it didn't. I looked at it a few times during the time I stayed there, to see if it would happen, but it didn't. It never came back again.

I don't know what the fuck that was. Maybe an over-active imagination. My mind likes to come up with lots of thoughts and ideas, whether or not they're useful or make sense. I think that sort of thing can make you mental, depending on how severe it is and what kind of environment you're in.

Fortunately, I managed to find a place to put my kind of mind to good use.

The Work Years

New Deal

I was almost 24. After about a year of sitting on my arse, I was ready to get a job. Any fucking job. I saw an advert for a shelf stacker in Lidl, which was £5 an hour. That was a lot of money to me, and I was thinking about it.

But then I went to the job centre one day to sign on, and I saw a sign on the desk for a New Deal course, where they'd teach you how to make websites, and I'd get something like an extra tenner a week on my giro. Plus there was a chance of a placement in a company at the end of it.

Aye, fuck it. I'd do that. I knew Photoshop and Illustrator and all these other things, but I didn't know how to make sites, and I didn't know how to get my foot in the door with a company.

I went to the course. It was in this wee business-centre place, and there were about a dozen people doing it. Some of them were only doing it for that extra bit of money on their giro, just spending their time on chatrooms. But I really wanted a job, I really wanted that placement. I listened to what these tutor folk were saying, I took it all in, I read up on stuff myself, I went up the Barras and got all the pirate software, and got tuned right into it. I was fucking gasping to get out of my situation.

Near the end of my course, which was eight weeks or something, I'd put together a wee portfolio of odds and ends that I'd made. I'd made some basic websites, I did some Photoshop stuff, general all-rounder things. It was enough for me to get a placement at a company called Black, these bigshots, maybe the best in Scotland. I was delighted.

I headed up there on my first day, and they were in this big fancy old-looking building called Speirs Wharf. They had about 20 staff, and I could hear English accents here and there, so I was thinking, 'English accents. This is big time.'

There wasn't much for me to do on that first day, or the second, but I got brought into a meeting once. I don't know why. I didn't know what to do. It was just for some of the staff, to talk about an up-and-coming project. There was a guy in a suit with a posh Scottish accent and moisturised skin. He said something about how the clients were 'major players'. It was the first time I'd heard all the wanky marketing patter. I felt right out of place. I felt like a daft wee ned. A wee council scheme ned, on a New Deal course.

At the end of the day I was invited out for a drink. It was a Friday and everybody was heading to a bar up the toon called the Candy Bar. It was only the second day in, and we're going out for a drink. That sounded very good to me. There were just a few of us to begin with, and I got chatting to them all. Then a few more dribbled in, and I got chatting with them. I felt good. I felt that these were people I could get on with, and I could become a part of this company and do well. I felt like I'd landed on my feet here.

A few more people came in, and they started talking about a fire. They said the building was on fire. The office.

I was like, 'What? What's that?'

A fire had started in Speirs Wharf, in the big building that the office was in. The fire brigade were there trying to put it out. It wasn't looking good, and everybody was worried, including me.

I was worried that they'd think it was me.

I honestly was.

I felt like I had 'CRIMINAL' on my forehead.

I was mainly worried about my placement, but I was partly worried that they'd think it was me. I saw it from their point of view. Everything was fine, until this strange guy turns up, this council scheme guy, and then there's a fucking fire.

I knew that nobody truly believed I started it, but you know what people are like. People are mental. They have thoughts that don't make any sense, a bit like the thoughts I was having at that moment. At the very least, they must surely be thinking, 'This guy is bad luck.'

When I turned up the next morning, I stood outside, along with a few other folk that worked there. You could see that there had been a fire up at the top, but our office was down on the ground floor. My boss showed up, and told me that the office was wrecked with water from the hoses all night. He said he'd been inside, and it was so bad that you could pour water out of the computers like they were teapots.

And until they knew what to do, there obviously wouldn't be a placement for me. He said he'd be in touch, hopefully, but he couldn't say when. Because this was pretty bad.

So that was that.

It looked very much like my hopes and dreams of working there were, dare I say it, pun intended, and I do apologise for this, but it looked like they were 'up in smoke'.

Haha!

But seriously, I was gutted.

Crossed Wires

I went back to that New Deal course, to finish the rest of it. The folk running it said they were sure that I'd be asked back to Black once they got themselves sorted, plus there were other companies interested. So I was quite optimistic.

But then I got into a situation that could have landed me in the jail.

In the course, I met this lassie. That's right, I nearly fucked things up over a lassie again. Not her fault. My fault. I'm a nutter.

I met this lassie that I fancied, and I had a feeling that she fancied me, but I couldn't be sure. I didn't know if we were being friendly or flirting or what. And anyway, she had a boyfriend, who would pick her up at the end of the day. So I was sure nothing would happen between us.

But then, one day, I said I was going to McDonald's, and she said she'd join me. It was a ten-minute walk, and I'd always go by myself, which she knew. So I wondered what was going on. Maybe she just fancied a McDonald's.

We chatted about nothing in particular. But then we went another few times, and she eventually mentioned her boyfriend. She said she was maybe going to break up with him, and I wondered if she was hinting that she was available. But I didn't know.

Anyway, the opportunity finally came to find out.

It was the end of the course, and we were all going out for a few drinks. There was about ten of us there, including her and me, and there was no boyfriend. I sat next to her, we got chatting, and I eventually got off with her. It felt like the ending of a long-running 'will they, won't they?' romcom.

But then I got fucking steaming.

I got fucking steaming, and fuck knows what sort of shite I was coming out with. But here's what I do remember. There was a gay guy there, a guy who was pals with one of the people on the course, and I asked if he had a flat. He did, and I asked if me and that lassie could come back. He said no, but I said I would maybe make it worth his while. As in, I hinted that I'd do something with him, just me and him. It was like I was trying to relive that time with my ex-girlfriend. Except this time I hadn't even asked the lassie if she fancied going.

He said aye, though, so I asked her. She said maybe, and we all walked to the train station. But by the time we got there, she'd changed her mind. I think she realised how wrecked I was. I was probably staggering. She just got on a train, so I went home, disappointed.

I woke up the next day, hungover, thinking back to how steaming I was. I was embarrassed. I still wanted to see her, though. We'd been getting on for ages, so maybe she would overlook how much of a mess I was on this one night.

So I emailed her. I had her Hotmail address from some previous New Deal-related email, a non-work address, and I emailed her to say that I was sorry for getting so wrecked and making a cunt of myself. I gave her my phone number, and said that if she ever leaves her boyfriend and fancies meeting up, even for a McDonald's, then text me or whatever. Sorry again for getting so pished.

A simple proposition, take it or leave it. But it turned out that I'd started a bit of a drama. She replied from her work address, saying, 'You shouldn't have emailed that address. That address is used by me and my boyfriend.'

I looked at the email address, and it was a combination of both their names with some number at the end. I thought, 'Oh fuck.' I hadn't noticed, because I'd never heard of a couple having a joint email address. What the fuck was that? The email went on to say that I'd caused her so much grief, and that they're still a couple.

So that was that. I'd blown it.

A couple of weeks passed, and I was kind of hoping for an email saying that she'd broken up with her boyfriend after all. But it never happened. Here's what did happen, though …

I started getting funny phone calls.

I'd hear a telly in the background for about a minute, and then somebody would shout some sound, like 'Blaaa!', then hang up. I'd check the number, but it was always withheld. I stopped answering, but I'd just get it in a voicemail, every few days.

It didn't take long for me to connect the dots. The boyfriend had a hold of my number, from that email, and he thought he'd wind me up, because I was this cunt that was trying to steal his bird.

He must have known I knew it was him. He must have enjoyed me knowing it was him, but not being able to do anything about it. Well, I could. I could smash his fucking motor up. I could go around to that New Deal building, hide outside, wait until he went in to pick her up, and then put his fucking windows in. He couldn't say it was me, because I had no reason to do it, unless he admitted he was provoking me with funny phone calls.

But I wasn't sure. Not 100 per cent. It could have been a coincidence, even though I had never got funny phone calls before, and I just so happened to get them within a week of me giving this cunt my number. Maybe it was just a coincidence.

Was it fuck.

So I emailed him.

I emailed that email address of theirs, and said, 'Here mate, you better stop giving me funny phone calls. You're playing with fire.'

I got a reply, but not from him. From her.

She said something like, 'What the fuck are you talking about? Psycho. He's not been giving you funny phone calls. Leave us alone.'

Fuck. What had I turned into?

Not that long ago, me and her were smiling at each other, going for walks. I got off with her and everything. And now I was a psycho, and I was to leave them alone. I had become one of these cunts you see in the news.

So I left it. I just left it. I'd given him the message, that was it.

I waited for the next funny phone call, but it didn't come. I'd been getting one every few days, and now it had been over a week, all since I sent that email.

So it was him after all, the wee prick. But that was it finished. The end.

Then, one night, I looked at my phone and I saw I had a missed call. It was a number I didn't recognise, but they'd left a voicemail.

I checked it, and it was him again. The telly in the background, then that 'Blaaaa!' at the end.

Obviously he'd stopped phoning for a while after getting my email, but he got the itch again. And he accidentally forgot to withhold his number. It was a stupid mistake. Maybe he got a drink in him.

A stupid, stupid mistake.

But I didn't know what to do about it. I wasn't the type to just phone the number and speak to him. I'm a bit of a shitebag when it comes to things like that. But I thought, right, I'm going to smash his motor. Or scratch it or something. If he went to the police, I'd be the prime suspect, but he'd have to admit to making nuisance phone calls. Would he get me arrested, knowing that he'd also be arrested? I didn't think so. I reckon I had him snookered.

But still, I wasn't 100 per cent sure it was him. So I had an idea of how to find out.

The number was a landline, and I reckoned this cunt still stayed with his mum and dad, because he was about 20 years old. What I'd do is I'd phone the number, and I'd ask for him by name, which was Keith, a slightly uncommon name. I'd say, 'Hi, is this Keith?' And if the voice said 'Aye,' or 'No, hold on and I'll get him,' then I'd hang up. Because that would be it confirmed. And his motor would be getting it later that week.

So I phoned the number. I didn't want to phone from my mobile and withhold my number, because it would look suspicious at his end and he might not answer it. So I went to a phone box instead, hoping that the number of the box would show up, which would look harmless.

It started ringing, and I was waiting to say, 'Hi, is that you, Keith?' My hands were shaking with adrenaline.

But it rang out, so I hung up.

I didn't try it again. The funny phone calls kept on coming, and I was floating between the options of ignoring him until he went away, or just doing in his motor without the confirmation. It was doing my nut in. I hadn't told any mates about it, because they'd probably think it was mental, the lengths I was going to.

But one night, a few weeks later, I was back in the Arches. I was having a drink and I was maybe eccied as well, and I bumped into a mate I hadn't seen for a while. He said to me, out of the blue, 'Here, have you been getting funny phone calls recently?'

I was surprised, because I hadn't told anycunt.

I was like, 'What? Aye, how d'you know about that?'

He laughed, and said it was him.

What?

I was standing there in the middle of the Arches, trying to understand what I'd just heard.

Take a moment to imagine how I felt. Close your eyes and imagine.

I said, 'But ... what? How ... when did ... what?'

He told me that he'd been wanting my phone number, so he asked a mutual mate a while back, and when he got my number he thought it would be funny to give me some funny phone calls.

I said, 'Wait a minute, wait, wait, wait.'

I almost didn't believe him. Even though the cunt was admitting it, I'd had it in my head for so long that it was this lassie's boyfriend, and I just couldn't adjust my thinking. I asked him to prove it. I asked him what the funny phone calls were, what he was supposedly doing.

He said he'd phone, then not say anything for a minute, then go 'Blaaaa!' at the end.

My fucking mind was blown.

My mind was blown not only because of that, but because of one other detail. See this mate of mine, this one who actually had been making the phone calls? Guess what his name was.

Keith.

I'm not making it up.

In other words, if his phone had been picked up that night that I phoned, and he'd said, 'Aye, this is Keith,' I would have been in jail before that week was out. The judge would have said, 'Get this madman off our streets.'

I am the luckiest cunt in the world. And also the unluckiest cunt in the world. What are the fucking chances of that happening?

But about that lassie …

I wondered what she thought about me, and if she saw me on the telly. I wondered if she was like that guy in the graveyard when I cut myself up. I pictured her pointing at the telly and saying, 'No way! That's that psycho I told you about, the one from the New Deal course! They gave him a fucking programme!' I was waiting for it to turn up in the papers or something.

But no, she sent me a friend request on Facebook.

I accepted and we got chatting. She was like, 'Long time no see!' and all that, and I asked her how she was keeping. She said nice things about the photos of my son. We exchanged all the usual pleasantries, like nothing had happened.

We even helped each other on FarmVille.

Flash

I'd like to talk to you now about Flash, and how it changed my life.

I know what you're wondering. 'Limmy, what's Flash?'

It's a piece of software.

'A piece of software changed your life? How come? Is it some sort of self-help app? Is it a mindfulness thing or something?'

No, it's a multimedia software platform used for creating animations and rich media applications.

'It's a what?'

Don't worry, you don't need to know the technical stuff. But I'll explain how this thing changed my fucking life. This was shortly after I turned 24.

I was eventually asked back onto that placement at Black. In there, they gave me these simple wee jobs, wee odd jobs like copying and pasting text into websites and slicing up graphics, just general donkey work. Bottom rung of the ladder work.

The thing is, even though it was simple work, I wasn't that good at it. I'd make wee mistakes here and there, because I'm sometimes not very good at following instructions. I'd never really noticed it before in college, but in a work environment where things were more rushed, my concentration would let me down. I wouldn't follow what somebody was saying, and I'd be too embarrassed to ask them to repeat it. I sometimes wouldn't remember things properly. I couldn't write it down, because I can't listen and write at the same time, fuck knows why. And I didn't want to ask each person to stop speaking every two seconds while I scribbled away. It would take ages.

I was a fucking mess.

It caused problems. I'd get funny looks. A few of the developers didn't have a lot of time for me. One of them snapped at me. He gave me these instructions that I didn't follow very well, and I had to ask him to repeat them a few minutes later. He reminded me, I said thanks, but then I had to go back to him again. He whipped off his headphones and said, 'Look, it's easy!', then showed me again, all pissed off.

It was fucking humiliating. I hated the way that cunt spoke to me, but what could I do? I couldn't say, 'Listen, I'm shite at this because this isn't how my brain works, give me something else,' because there wasn't something else. There was nothing else I could do.

But then I saw Flash.

Back in late 1998 most websites did nothing. They were static – just words and pictures, like online brochures with links to take you between the pages. But there was a thing called Flash, Macromedia Flash 3, that let you do all these animations, these big, full-screen animations, things that looked like videos or cartoons or arty title sequences, with sounds and music and everything. You made it in Flash, the user installed the Flash plug-in for their browser to view it, and that was it. It looked fucking amazing.

I'd seen it used by other companies, but Black wasn't using it much at the time. So I installed it on my computer and started teaching myself how to use it, looking at tutorials and things like that. I felt like I was good at it, good at animating stuff, good at coming up with wee ideas for animations, abstract stuff, interface stuff, buttons, galleries, interesting things to look at. I was fucking desperate to be good at something, because I hated all that other work, and I still hadn't been offered a job yet. I didn't want to get kicked out at the end of the placement.

I showed one of my bosses what I'd been doing, and he liked it. He suggested that I could make an interactive map for Black's new website, which I did. He liked that as well; a few people did. They were like, 'Oooh, nice.' What a fucking joy to hear that. And it got better. We all went out for a few drinks, and one of the boss's pals got chatting to me, some guy with a hi-fi company. He said he loved the wee map I did, and wondered if I could do something like that for him. My boss said no homers were allowed, but I was buzzing to be asked.

I know that maybe sounds pathetic to you, but it was maybe the first time I'd ever felt in demand. All because of this daft wee fucking map.

I was then asked to do the intro animation for the new site. And then there was some other animation I was asked to do. And I was getting brought into meetings and getting asked by these bosses in suits if I had any ideas of how to jazz up some website or another. I'd come up with ideas, and they'd be nodding and smiling.

I got offered a full-time job. It was something like £11,000 a year, which was fuck all, but it was fucking megabucks to me. And the main thing was that I had a job. An actual full-time job, my first ever fucking job. And I liked it, and I was good at it.

In early 1999, three or four months after being this wee dafty getting snapped at for not knowing how to submit websites to search engines, I was the main Flash cunt in there. I got asked to do my first full website, for this new dance festival called Homelands. I built all that, we got VIP tickets to go to the thing, and I was at the festival, knowing that I'd built the website, watching Underworld, my favourite band at the time. I was on top of the fucking world.

They gave me a pay rise, and asked me to build more sites for clubs and radio stations and wee viral playthings to promote stuff, lots of stuff, lots and lots of ideas. I had plenty of them, lots and lots and lots. The perfect fucking job. Finally. Finally, I found what I was good at. Coming up with ideas for stuff and making them.

But I also fancied making something of my own. I had these ideas for funny wee playthings, but there was nowhere to put them. So I made a website called Limmy.com.

At that time, there were other Flash developers that had their own personal sites, but their stuff tended to be all arty or thoughtful or abstract and experimental. I wanted to do the opposite. I wanted my stuff to be technically clever, but fucking stupid, and funny.

I made it so that when you came to the site, techno started blaring, and there was me down the bottom right in this never-ending video loop, dancing, facing the camera with this stupid look on my face, like an old-school entertainer. And the menu linked off to these two wee things I made.

One was called Scream If You Wanna Go Faster, which was made like it was a soundboard for people who worked at the shows, like the waltzers. There were wee animations of the rides, and buttons you could press to hear me hit out with lines like 'Get on the outside, the left side's the fast side!' and 'Please guys, play it safe, don't jump on when we're moving!' All said in that mid-Atlantic accent they tended to put on.

The other plaything was called Come Again, which was basically an arty shagging machine.

I posted the site onto a few forums, to see what people would say. They thought it was hilarious, or mental. I'd read the comments and I'd be all excited. People were saying my nickname, people were saying 'Limmy'. They were talking about me.

I checked my analytics to see how many people were looking at it, and it was a mammoth 300 people a day. That's fuck all compared to these days, but back then that felt like most of the world. I could see that there were people checking it down south and over in America, and all over the world. I wondered who they were and how they saw it and what they thought.

Now that I knew people were watching me, it spurred me on to make some more stuff to add to the collection. People would talk about me more. They thought I was clever and funny and mental and interesting and, ohhhh, I loved it. I loved what was happening to me.

And it was all because of Flash.

Sexual Explosion

My confidence was sky high. I was doing well, and getting paid for it. I was finally ready to be a man about town and go shagging about like a normal person. Here are some examples of what I got up to. I say 'examples', like this is just a small selection, but this is pretty much the full list. It isn't long.

Lassie I Knew from School

I was pals with this lassie in fifth year, and we were wondering back then who would lose their virginity first. She did, when she was 16, and she started shagging about. I liked how she shagged about like that, 'like a guy'. Nothing happened between us back then, but whenever we bumped into each other, there seemed to be something between us. And when I bumped into her again while I had this job, she said we had 'unfinished business'.

We got off with each other to begin with. She had this big tongue, a big forceful tongue that I liked, just going for it down my throat. We got off with each other, and we just hung about, going to pubs and having a laugh. Then we talked about maybe going back to mine and having a shag. I said I wasn't sure, because I really liked her and I didn't want anything to change between us. I'd have been happy to be her boyfriend or something, but I didn't want to ruin this pally thing we always had. It would be a fucking shame if we lost it. She promised me that nothing would change, and I said that if she broke her promise I'd never forgive her.

We went back to mine and had a shag. She said to me, 'You're wee, but you're game as fuck.' I thought that was alright, more positive than negative. Then she left the next day.

A day or so later I gave her a phone to see if she fancied a drink the following night. We'd been meeting up like that every few days, and we'd been having a laugh. But this time when I phoned her she was different. She spoke slower, with a kind of smile in her voice.

She said, 'Oh, I don't know. Hmmm, nah. Maybe another day.'

I said to her, 'What d'you mean? D'you not want to meet up?'

She said, 'No, I do. Just … hmmm … I'll see how I feel. Maybe, maybe not.'

You might think that sounds flirty and playful, but the way I felt at the time, I kind of felt my heart breaking. I wasn't upset about whether or not she wanted to be my girlfriend or if she wanted a shag. I wasn't that interested in that, really. I was thinking about our friendship. We'd bumped into each other for years and we'd always been happy to see each other, and we were cheeky with each other. We were mates. She was like this mate that I loved, and something had changed.

I said, 'You've changed. This is what I was scared of. You said you wouldn't change, you promised.'

She said, 'Well, that's women for you.'

And I think I just hung up.

She phoned back a few days later, and I ignored her. She messaged and I ignored her. I just wanted to forget it and move on. A friendship fucking ruined. I didn't want any of that mind-game stuff.

I bumped into her in a pub one Saturday night in Shawlands a year or so later. She was drunk and calling me a bastard, in this jokey sort of way. She kept coming up to my face and blowing a raspberry, inches from my face. We had this wee argument, kind of light-hearted, but an honest argument, where I told her that she broke my fucking heart, it was all her fault, we had something good.

She asked me if I fancied one last kiss. And I did. But I just said no, no way. I wanted to deny her something, because of what she denied me. She denied me a good pal that I had for years. Then she went away.

I've bumped into her a few times between then and now, and we get on. I'm always happy to see her, even to just see her on Facebook. She's got big smiling eyes and a big smiling face, just like she always did when we were pals.

Lassie Up the Toon

One night I went back to this lassie's flat. I don't know how I met her – I can't remember talking to her in a club or out on the street – but I went back with her and we shagged. No lick-outs, gobbles or wanks, just a no-frills missionary shag in the dark. I remember her pulling my arse towards her a bit faster than I was shagging, to get me to speed up. Neither of us came.

I woke up the next day and I saw that she was a uni student, sharing a flat with her uni pals. I got her number, then I left.

I fancied another shag, so I messaged her a few days later and asked if she fancied meeting up. She said she didn't think I'd get in touch, but aye, alright. I went over to her flat, and we chatted, with me talking a lot of shite and her laughing. Then we turned off the light and we had another shag, in the same sort of way as before. Then I stayed the night.

We met up a few times like that, with me going over there. She told me that she was now going on the Pill, seeing as she was shagging more often. I said, 'Wait a minute, so you weren't on the Pill that first night? I didn't have a johnny on, you could have got pregnant.' She said, 'Well, it didn't stop you.' Which was a good point.

One night I gave her a phone, to see what she was up to. She said she was having a night out. I said, 'Oh, who you with?', wondering if it was the sort of thing I could go along to.

She said, 'That's none of your business,' but not in a serious way.

I said, 'No, I was just wondering if you're out with your mates or whatever.'

She said she was. So I asked if she fancied me coming along. But she said something like, 'Em … if you want.' Something that sounded like, 'If you must.'

I said, 'Och, it's fine, I'm actually knackered,' and told her to enjoy her night, something like that.

I didn't know what the conversation meant, exactly. By saying to me, 'That's none of your business,' was she reminding me that I wasn't her boyfriend and had no right to ask that? Did she want me to be her boyfriend? Or did she not?

I didn't know. But I saw it as her keeping me at arm's length. I was just for shagging.

I met up with her another couple of times. But then one night I texted her, and she said that I was just using her for sex.

I thought we were both using each other for sex. I thought about what my old college pal said to me when I had that evil presence. So I replied with, 'You're just using me for sex.'

But we didn't meet up after that.

No more sex.

Lassie That Was Shagging My Mate

There was a lassie I knew for a while from the pubs I went to, a lassie I fancied, who had been shagging one of my mates on and off. I got off with her one night, but nothing came of it. But then about six months later we met up again. We went back to a flat I was looking after for a workmate while he was away on holiday.

We got off with each other, and I gave her a lick-out. Then we shagged for a bit. Neither of us came. Then we fell asleep, and parted company in the morning. Neither of us were that interested in each other.

She went back to shagging my mate for a while. He told me she said I was shite at giving lick-outs. I asked him what she said about the shagging, and she said I was 'alright'.

Two Lassies and a Boyfriend

There was a lassie I'd fancied for ages, a lassie I'd never been involved with because she had a boyfriend. She would come out with all this sexual patter, asking what I thought of her arse in the clothes she was wearing, because she knew I liked her arse. We were kind of open about all that. There were never any actual come-ons between us when we were alone, but I had a million wanks imagining a million scenarios.

Then, one night, we were out in a club, her boyfriend was there, and so was this lassie we knew. Her and this lassie started getting off with each other. Then her boyfriend gets off with the lassie. Then I get off with the lassie. Then I get off with the one that I'd fancied for ages. It just all kind of happened. I remember looking at the dancefloor and seeing a couple of lassies looking over, stunned. I waved at them, and they ran away.

At the end of the night we left the club, with me going to get a taxi, and them heading home. I eventually got a taxi, and I was almost home when I saw that I had two voicemail messages. I listened to one, and it was the lassie's boyfriend saying that I should head over to his, and I could hear the two lassies in the background sounding like they were doing something sexual. It was 'Uhhhh! Uhhhh!'

I thought, 'Bullshit. What?!'

Then I checked the next message, and it was the lassie that I fancied. She said 'Limmy. This is your one and only chance. Get over here.' It was like one of these stories I'd read in the porno mags, but it was happening.

I told the driver to take me to the 24-hour garage, because I needed to get johnnies, and I'd be heading back the way I came to a foursome. The driver was all excited for me, like he couldn't wait to tell his taxi driver mates.

I got to the flat and asked the lassie's boyfriend if this was for real, and he said aye. I went to the bedroom, and there they were in bed, lying about with no clothes on. I can't remember what I said to the lassies. Probably, 'Fucking hell, look at this.'

I took my clothes off, a bit self-conscious at my lack of a hard-on. I took a swig of the bottle of Aftershock that was nearby, for a bit of courage, even though I was already steaming. I got into bed, and this lassie, the one that I'd fancied for ages, starts giving me a gobble.

But I couldn't get a hard-on.

She had my wee soft willy in her mouth, occasionally pulling it, but nothing was happening. I was like, 'Fuck's sake.' Her boyfriend was doing things with the other lassie, he obviously didn't mind, but it was maybe all too much for me.

I got a wee bit harder, just a semi. In fact, less than a semi. A quarter. And I tried to put a johnny on it. Then she pulled me onto her to try and shag her. But I just fucking couldn't.

Me and the other lassie tried kissing, but fuck all happened. The lassie that I fancied was on all fours for a second, in a pose that looked right out of the magazines that I wanked over. I put my finger to her arsehole, but she pulled away and said, 'No you don't. Not even he gets to do that.'

I just couldn't fucking get a hard-on. There was a moment when her boyfriend leaned over and held my cock, then let go. It was a funny kind of moment. He didn't give it a tug; he just put his hand around it, then let go. But that didn't do anything either.

Then her and her boyfriend put their clothes on and went to another room to go to sleep. My one and only chance with this lassie I'd had a million wanks over was gone.

The funny thing is, me and the other lassie ended up shagging when they went away. I shagged her with a full hard-on. Not a semi. A full hard-on. And I didn't even fancy her.

When we met up the day after, none of us spoke about it. We weren't embarrassed. We just didn't speak about it, ever.

Lassie at the Launch Party

One night I was at a launch party for something, and I ended up getting off with a lassie I knew, despite there usually being no sexual chemistry between us. I think we were just bored. When she said she was heading home, I asked if I could come, and she said alright.

When we got back, she said she was going to have a bath. I asked if I could join her, and she laughed it off and said that she didn't think that would work, but alright, if I wanted to. She was already in the bath, and I stripped off and got in at the other side. That would have been unthinkable in the old days, to just strip off in front of a lassie I didn't know in that way, with my floppy cock, and get in a bath. But I was on top of the world, so I didn't care. She said something about how I needed to go to a gym, because of my belly. I said I didn't care about all that.

We didn't do anything in the bath, but when we dried off we went into the bedroom and I tried to shag her. I kissed her for a bit, but I couldn't be arsed with giving her a lick-out or poking her or anything like that. So when I tried to shag her, my hard-on just bumped up against what felt like a clenched fist. I didn't know if she was tightening herself up, or if it was because I hadn't made her wet, or what. But I just left it at that, rolled over, and we went to sleep.

We got up the next morning, and we were chatting in her flat. There was no chemistry between us again, if there ever had been. Then I left.

The next weekend a crowd of us were out having a drink, and she was there. And I could see that she was telling folk about that night. She was sitting a few seats away, and some folk were looking at me and going 'Ooooooh!', something like that.

She then wagged her pinky, to suggest I had a wee cock, and that got a laugh.

I said, 'Aye right. More like this …' And I took my middle finger and tried inserting it into my clenched fist, with it bouncing off the entrance because it wouldn't fit.

She went quiet. Then the subject was changed.

I don't know if I overstepped the mark, but she started it.

Three Lassies in One Bed

I ended up back at a flat, with some guys and lassies I knew. People started leaving, but a few were told they were allowed to sleep over if they wanted, on the couch. But I went into the bedroom, stripped off to my pants, switched off the light, and got into bed.

Three lassies came into the room, one of which I knew well, and she said, 'Limmy, get out, we're sleeping in there.'

I said, 'Oh, c'mon, plenty of room.' If I got asked again, I would have got out, but nobody said anything. They just went away, and didn't come back until a good while later.

Two of them came in, and slept beside me. I kept my distance a bit. I was wondering if I'd feel a hand reach over and touch me, but it didn't happen. I think they fell asleep.

Then another lassie came in, the one that I knew. She got in beside me, and she started touching me. We got off with each other for a while, then I was lying on her, wondering if we were actually going to shag, next to her pals.

She pushed me down, under the covers, for me to give her a lick-out. I was down there for a while, and I remember it being very wet, either her fanny wet by itself, or with my slabbers, or both. But it went on for fucking ages, with her holding on to my head. My face was sweaty because it was roasting. I didn't like it. I regretted getting into that bed.

Eventually she came, I think. She stopped moving about. So I moved my head back up to the pillow. I thought we were maybe going to shag, but she just turned around and went to sleep.

We all woke up the next day and had breakfast, and nothing was said about the lick-out. I was half expecting her to say, 'Well, I thought if he was going to sleep in my bed, he could make himself useful, hahaha. Isn't that right, Limmy?'

I bumped into her about a year later, and she said she was applying to be on *Big Brother*. For her audition video, she said it starts with her walking out of her toilet and up to the camera, where she says, 'I'd give it a minute in there.'

I thought about her doing a smelly shite, and that time I got pushed down to that vicinity to lick her fanny, before she rolled over and went to sleep.

It made me feel quite feminine.

Sexy Designer

There was a lassie in my work, a designer, who I'd fancied from day one. She was tanned, dark hair, these big blue eyes. I could hardly contain how much I fancied her. Whenever she spoke to me, I'd go a bit shy, or I'd be a bit distant or unfriendly to disguise how I felt. She was kind of cool, and I was this wee ned guy, and I didn't want to give her the creeps by showing that I fancied her. She was miles out of my league.

I started treating her badly. I thought she thought she was better than me. I'd say to folk that I didn't rate her as a designer. I'd be all cold with her when we went out for drinks. We had a Christmas night out and there was this wee food fight, and I specifically went for her, throwing sprouts her way. I reverted to nasty, primary school behaviour.

There was another guy in work that didn't like her, for some reason, and he started a bit of a bullying campaign against her. He was an older guy, a developer, and he'd bad-mouth her or do annoying things. I went along with it, agreeing with the things he said.

But I started working with her on certain jobs, which I hadn't really done before, with her designing stuff and me building it. And I liked her. I liked just talking with her. She was sharp and funny. By that point I had a lot more confidence than I did at the start of working there, due to me getting good at my job, and me shagging about. I didn't have that inferiority thing eating away at me and making me an absolute prick.

A lot of us went to the Homelands dance festival again, this time in 2000. She was there, as well as the guy who had it in for her. We were in one of the tents, and he just stood there staring at her, in an intimidating way, wherever she went. I asked him what he was doing, and he said he was trying to freak her out. I thought that was out of order, and I asked him to give her a break, which he did. I felt bad about the lot of it. I'd been a fucking monster to her.

A week or so later I told her about Homelands, and what I said to that guy, and things changed between me and her. I know I've got a cheek trying to tell this as some kind of redemption story, where I treat this lassie like shite, then I stop and I want a medal for it. But I changed, and so did things between me and her.

When we all went out for drinks after work, I'd have a laugh with her. I remember somebody brought a camera out, then they showed pictures afterwards, and she was pulling these funny faces that I hadn't seen her do before. And I thought that she was fucking brilliant.

She came out one night, wearing these tight bottoms, some sort of stretchy trousers. And it was the first time I'd seen her arse. My fucking jaw dropped. From the side, there was this vertical line of her back and legs, and in between was this perfect semi-circle of her arse that stuck out from it. I'd already had a million wanks over her, but I had a billion more. Thinking about that arse. I was fucking gobsmacked.

I heard she had broken up with her boyfriend. And one night when we were all out for drinks I got off with her. It was like the end of a long journey. It was something that was previously unthinkable.

Around that time, me and a few others from that company had decided to leave and start up our own. Me and her went back to my office one night, and we shagged. It was a dream come true. We met up a few more times for a shag, and we got more into it. Things got a bit more rough and athletic. I'd never been like that before, and it was the first time I came while shagging. I'd never come before through shagging, I'd always just stopped because it didn't seem to be going anywhere.

It was after one particular shag that I asked her, 'So, are we going out then?' I think my cock was still inside her at the time. She said aye.

And we've been together ever since.

That sexy designer is my girlfriend Lynn McGowan. We've been together for 18 years, and we've got a son who is eight.

She has asked me to not talk any more about our private life, in particular the ups and downs of our sex life. But I suppose I can sum things up with an example from back then before we started officially going out.

On that very first night, when we headed back to my office for a shag, the first thing I did wasn't to rip off her clothes and grab her arse and stick my tongue right up it and shag the living daylights out of her. The first thing I did was to go onto my computer and check out a few forums, check to see what was happening in the Flash community.

Becoming an Alky

My confidence was sky high. Perhaps too high. I started to feel indispensable. So much so that I had a fight with one of my bosses. An actual scrap.

One Friday night, a group of us from work all headed out to the pub for a few drinks. We went to the Candy Bar, which was the same pub I went to with my work when I just started my placement, that night of the fire. Back when I started my placement, I was all sheepish and eager to make a good impression. But this was a year later, and I was fucking steaming.

I didn't like this boss. I didn't hate him, but I didn't like him. He was one of the suits, one of the account managers, one of the guys that pitched to the clients and brought the money in. I'd hear him talk about money and clients, huge amounts of money, then he'd come over to me and ask me to do some work. Then he'd drive off at the end of the day in his sports motor while I grafted away doing all-nighters for £13,000 a year or whatever I was on.

I didn't like how he sometimes made jokes about me getting sacked. I'd mention how I nearly made a mistake with a certain website or something, and he'd chuckle and say that would have been a 'career-ender', or 'an interesting way to get your P45'. He had a point, but I didn't like how it was implied that he could get me sacked, and that he had that power.

To be honest, though, my reasons for not liking him were even smaller than that. I didn't like the way he looked around the office on his way from the printer room to his desk, surveying his kingdom. I didn't like overhearing his laugh; I imagined he was laughing at the expense of somebody like me. I didn't like that when I talked to him he sometimes looked at my hair. He was one of those cunts that look at your hair or some other part of you while you're speaking to him, like he's wearing sunglasses and you won't notice.

He once said something about how I was getting a bit of a beer belly. When he said that, I didn't mind, for some reason. But it was this other night, at the Candy Bar, that he said something that I did mind about. And it was nothing. It was something like, 'Interesting T-shirt.'

Ten seconds later, we had each other in a headlock.

I can't remember how it happened exactly, but I think it was because I said, 'Interesting tie,' and started flicking his tie in response. Then he pushed my hand away, so I slapped his away from mine. Fuck knows. But I remember us having each other in a headlock in the middle of this pub.

One of my colleagues grabbed me from behind in a bear hug, so my arms were pinned by my side, and he dragged me out of the pub. I asked him what the fuck he was doing. He told me he was doing it for my own good, and that I should go home. He told the bouncers not to let me back in, then went back inside.

I didn't want to go fucking home, so I went to walk back in, but the bouncers stopped me. I asked them why they were barring me, it wasn't them who chucked me out, it was my workmate, but they told me to forget it.

I hung about a bit, waiting for the bouncers to get distracted. They eventually took their eyes off me, so I tried to run past them. They grabbed me and shoved me back out. They really fucking grabbed me, and really shoved me, like they took pleasure in it. So I was like that to one of them, 'What the fuck are you doing?'

Then I tried to punch his jaw.

The pair of them grabbed me and punched into my head, before chucking me back onto the pavement. I felt my head, then looked at my hand, and there was blood. I don't know how they did it, but I was bleeding.

I was like that, 'That's it, I'm phoning the polis. That's assault.' I was nearly crying.

I phoned 999, right in front of them, to scare them. The police asked me what the emergency was. I said that I'd been chucked out of a pub and the bouncers had battered me. The person on the phone told me that wasn't an emergency and told me to not waste their time. I had to hang up in front of the bouncers, humiliated.

Two policemen happened to walk up the street anyway, and I told them what had happened. I said that these two bouncers here did this to me. The bouncers said that I threw the first punch. The police asked if that was true, and I said aye, but look at the state of me, officer. The police said that if I really wanted to pursue it, I could go to the station and give a statement, but it would mean a trial and all the rest of it. So I just fucking left it. I felt like they'd got away with murder.

One of my colleagues came out and saw the state of me. She took me down to a public toilet to get washed. I saw my face in the mirror and it was covered in blood. I was a fucking shambles, and I was dizzy as fuck. It was like concussion or something.

When I left the toilet, she told me to go home, and I said I would, and left her.

But instead, I headed for a club, by myself. I headed to The Arches.

I got to the door, and I was expecting the bouncers to give me an instant knock-back, due to me being wrecked. But instead, they gave me a wee search. They were about to let me in, but then they lifted up my hands to look at them. I forgot to wash the back of my hands, and they were still covered in blood. The bouncer put both hands on my shoulders, turned me around 180 degrees, and gave me a wee push.

I didn't bother arguing. The night was over.

I stopped a taxi and got in, and told him where I was heading. Carnwadric, on the south side of Glasgow.

I was in a cunt of a mood.

The driver didn't look like he was heading south, so I started saying, 'Where the fuck's this? What way's this, the scenic route?' I've never used that patter before. I have never spoken to a driver like that before. I'd heard that 'scenic route' patter, and I just wanted to use it. I just wanted to be the cheekiest, most horrible cunt out. I was almost acting.

The driver told me that because of the one-way system up the toon, he had to go this way to go that way.

I was like, 'My fucking arse. You're a fucking conman, mate.'

The driver stopped the taxi and told me to get out. I told him I wasn't fucking getting out, and he had to take me where I wanted to go. He told me that if I didn't get out then he was taking me to the police station. I told him to fucking take me to the fucking police fucking station, so fucking fuck.

Then I fell asleep.

The next thing I knew, I was waking up to the sound of him shutting his door. I looked out and I could see him crossing the road to a police station in Cowcaddens, and walking in.

I shat it.

I went to open the door, but it was locked. So was the one on the other side. He'd locked me in.

I was going to get fucking jailed.

After keeping out of trouble for so long, I was about to get fucking jailed and lose everything.

The taxi was a black Hackney, so there was a barrier between me and the front seats. I was going to kick it the fuck in and press whatever button got me out of the taxi, and maybe knock some money into the bargain.

But then I tried the window, the one on the passenger door. It was the kind with a metal rim that you grabbed to slide right down. And that's what it did.

I jumped out the window, and fell onto the road. Then I ran onto the pavement, jumped over a fence and hid in a hedge. Then I waited a few seconds, and ran like fuck.

I didn't know what to do. My house was five miles away, I couldn't be fucked walking, I couldn't be fucked getting a bus, but I couldn't get another taxi. The driver would probably be telling all the other drivers to keep on the lookout, and that if I got in one of their taxis they were to phone the police and hand me over. In fact, if I walked home they'd maybe take the law into their own hands. Maybe drive me away somewhere and knock fuck out of me with truncheons.

I walked for a few minutes, thinking about how I was going to stay in the shadows for the duration of the five-mile walk.

Then I saw a taxi and thought, 'Fuck it.' I put out my hand, and got in. And got home no bother.

When I woke up the next day and remembered what I done, especially the fight with my boss, I thought, 'Oh no.' I thought I'd fucked it. Completely fucked it. I was getting the sack. Definitely getting the sack.

I typed up an email to apologise. A big one, then I made it shorter, then I made it longer. I said something in it along the lines of 'I've got a problem.' It was like an alcoholic low point. But I ended up not sending it and just speaking to the guy in person. He was always one of the first in, just like me, so I made sure I came in early on the Monday.

I said I was so, so fucking sorry, so sorry.

He just laughed it off and said it was fine, don't worry about it.

That was pretty decent of him, wasn't it?

No, it wasn't. People like him enabled my behaviour. My drunken behaviour got worse. And it's because of people like him. It's all his fault, not mine. What a cunt.

No, I'm joking. But my drinking did get worse.

Being an Alky

I started having pub lunches on an almost daily basis. I'd have a pint, sometimes two, and on the rare occasion, three. This was about the same time as when I had that week-long hangover I told you about, the one where I shat myself.

A few of us would go for these pub lunches sometimes, and the bosses didn't like it. It wasn't so much the drinking as us taking the full hour away from our desk. They'd have had us eating our lunch while working, if they'd had it their way. So we started getting an attitude on us, and a few of us decided to leave and start our own company. We didn't leave just because of the pub lunches. We mainly left because we didn't feel appreciated, and we thought we could do it ourselves. But privately, I was also thinking about the pub lunches. I wanted the freedom to do what I wanted, to come and go as I pleased.

When we started trying to get work in, I realised that having my own company wasn't going to be the holiday that I thought. I was one of the three bosses in our three-man business, and I was expected to do more than just Flash work. I was expected to do boss things, like make phone calls, or go to meetings. I didn't like it, I wasn't good at it. I wasn't good at doing normal things like that. I was used to sitting there and coming up with ideas, not actually speaking to potential clients in my phone voice.

I felt like a wean. I kind of was a wean compared to the other two; I was about four or five years younger than them. I felt like a teenager, despite being almost 26. And I acted like a teenager. I started using the office as a place to crash after being out on the piss. I remember one of my colleagues coming in when I'd been sleeping under a desk, and me trying to have a wee laugh about it. But one of them spoke to me privately about it, about that and other things. He said that if I continued to not pull my weight, then he'd ask the other director to leave the company with him and start a new one. I shat myself. What the fuck would I do if he did that? Go back to Black with my tail between my legs and ask for my old job back?

I felt like I was on borrowed time, but every now and then there would be a wee reminder of what I contributed to the company. One day I got an email from this bigshot design magazine called *Creative Review*, an email to Limmy.com, saying that they liked my stuff and that they were considering me for some new talent award called Creative Futures. That gave me a boost. I told the person about my company and the work we'd collectively done, and our company got the award, and we went down to London for some big exhibition thing. I kept telling myself, 'That was me that did that.'

We began to employ more people until there were seven of us, including another director, and things got better. But about a year after we'd started the company, three of the four directors decided to leave and start up another new company, due to some personality clashes with the remaining director. Ironically, it wasn't me being left behind, but the one who threatened to leave me behind when we had that private chat. I'd like to tell you it was some kind of revenge plot a year in the making, but it wasn't. We wanted him out, but he wouldn't budge, so we had to start a new company from scratch.

It was scary. We had hardly any work, and we were competing with our old company. Lynn had left Black to go freelance, and she was going through a period of getting fuck-all work. We were skint. We'd moved in together, and now we had just enough money for two months' rent. I was thinking, 'What have I fucking done?' I remember me and Lynn sitting in Yates's Wine Lodge one rainy afternoon, depressed as fuck, not knowing what to do.

But things picked up. We started getting some work in, we employed an extra guy so there were four of us, but then one of the directors left, then the designer left. Until it was just me and the other director, Donnie. We'd be talking about how we were going to get work in, and what the consequences would be if we didn't, and how if things kept up the way they were going, we were fucked. We'd also be having a laugh. Donnie's one of the funniest cunts in the world. But he's also a very sensible cunt. And he'd worked out that unless X, Y and Z happened, we were fucked.

I think it was about that time, which was about three years into the company in 2004, that I really started drinking. I was 29 at this point.

I was back to the pub lunches on an almost daily basis. A large red wine, every time. It gave me a wee buzz when I got back to the office, it was almost medicinal. Then, on the cycle home, I'd nip into a pub or two, by myself. A wee pint here or another red wine there. Then, when I got home, I'd maybe have half a bottle of red wine, or maybe just finish the lot. I'd just sit in bed watching the same film over and over, the Alfred Hitchcock film *Rope*.

I'd still be able to get on with my work, but sometimes I couldn't be fucked, and I'd just put it off till the next day, or the weekend. I remember there was some work I was supposed to have finished by one particular Friday, but I couldn't be bothered, so I planned to go in on the Sunday so it was finished by Monday.

When the Sunday came, Lynn said she wanted to go into the toon and spend an afternoon with me, having a drink, getting lunch, going to the pictures. I told her that I had to go into work because I didn't get stuff finished, and she was pissed off. I said it hopefully wouldn't take long.

As I was cycling to work, I passed this pub on King Street with a live jazz band playing inside. I'd been in before, and I liked it. The pub had these big windows, and from the outside you could see all these older folk up dancing to this upbeat jazz. It was very inviting. There was me on my way to work, on a Sunday, and there were these people living it up.

I thought I'd pop in for one. Just the one.

I went in and got a pint of heavy, which I'd started taking a liking to. I watched the band and the people dancing. This was the life. I just wanted to soak it up a bit before I went to work.

When I finished that pint, I thought I'd get another. It was hard to drag myself away. But I'd leave after that.

Then I got a third pint. And I made the decision that I wasn't going to go into work. I'd catch up on Monday, and maybe stay late. I just didn't want to leave. I had a pint and a seat and all this liveliness around me, it was like a jazz funeral, the upbeat bit. It was like a wee corner of heaven.

I thought I should phone Lynn and get her round. I phoned her and said that I wasn't going in to work after all, and she should come round to this pub, because there was this band playing. She obviously couldn't believe her ears. I'd cancelled her plans in order to go in to work, then I ended up just going to the pub myself. We had an argument, and she hung up.

Good. I'll just get another pint in.

I stayed for a few more, then I phoned her back, asking if she fancied going to the pictures. We had another argument, but she eventually said alright, and that she'd pick me up at Argyle Street.

I left, and walked up. But I reckoned I had another five minutes or so to spare. So I went into another pub, and ordered a quick drink. I fancied a White Russian, for some reason. I never got that. But I ordered a pint, and practically downed it.

She eventually picked me up, and we started driving. I kept my mouth shut to avoid an argument. But after a while I started speaking, about nothing in particular. Lynn realised just how steaming I was, and said that she wasn't going to go to the pictures with me like that. She was going to turn the car around and head home. We got into another argument, and I said to her, 'Oh for fuck's sake, Lynn, why have you got to be such a *bastard*?'

She just pulled over to the side of the road and said, 'Get out.' And I got out.

She must have felt that I was a right waste of her time. A waste of her life. But I didn't care. I cared a bit, but not enough. And I still don't. What I mean is, whatever it is that prevents the average person from becoming an alky, whether it's pride or decency or common sense or restraint or impulse control or remorse or just plain old fucking happiness, I don't have it. I'm trying to imagine how she must have felt, and I can't. I can say the words, but I don't feel it. When I got kicked out the motor, there was the feeling that I'd done something wrong, that I'd drunk too much. But now I'd been given the opportunity to drink some more.

I headed over to my office, which wasn't too far away. I didn't do any work. We had all this free booze lying about due to us doing the website for Kronenbourg 1664. I just got more drunk on that, then got a taxi home.

That was another thing I got back into doing. Using the office as a place to crash after being out on the piss.

One night, me and Lynn were out having a drink, a Friday or Saturday night, and I bumped into somebody I knew, this lassie who said she was going to a party. I asked her if we could invite ourselves along later, and she said aye. She told us where it was, and left.

Lynn wasn't into going, but I said it would be good. We'd get a bottle of wine to bring along, and there would be plenty of booze there. I went to a shop and got a bottle, but we couldn't find the party. Lynn wanted to head home, but I said I was staying out to find this party, and she left by herself.

I walked about, but I couldn't find it, so I just headed back to my office, which was nearby. And I sat up all night on Yahoo Chat, while I got pished on this bottle of wine.

I woke up the next morning, near midday, and messaged Lynn to say that I was on my way back. I can't remember what she replied with, but she didn't ask me to come back right away, so I got the feeling that there was no rush. When I left the office, I thought I'd pop into a nearby pub for a drink. I was hungover, and having a drink when I was hungover felt good. So I had one.

Then another.

I got a train to Bridgeton, which was where we were staying. I started walking home, which was only five minutes away, but I fancied going into one of these old man's pubs in Bridgeton that I'd never been into. So I went in for one.

Then another.

And another.

I wasn't getting messaged from Lynn asking me where I was and telling me to hurry up, so I reckoned it was alright.

So I had another.

I didn't realise how drunk I was until I tried making conversation with somebody. I was playing a fruit machine, and a guy said something to me. I tried to say something funny back, but it came out as a slur. I couldn't speak, and he walked away.

But I wasn't too slurry to get another drink.

A while later, about late afternoon, Lynn was heading round to the shops. (She told me this the next day.) She headed round to the shops, at Bridgeton Cross, and she saw some alky guy sitting under the Bridgeton Cross Shelter, eating a curry. He was eating it straight out of the containers, and the curry was all over his shirt. Then, of course, she realised it was me.

She went to the shops, got some stuff and went back home herself, like she didn't know me. I was oblivious, with my curry.

She said I came home and went to the toilet. Then I never came out. She knocked on the door, but I didn't answer. She had to unlock the door from the outside, and there I was on the floor, conked out. I'd been sick in the bath. Red wine, lager and curry sick.

That was a low point for me. But not low enough.

I'd done tons of stuff like that. I conked out in the toilet of a restaurant, steaming, and the waiter had to unlock the cubicle door and wake me while I had my trousers around my ankles. Another time, I was at Lynn's granny and grandad's anniversary party, wrecked, and I was cheeky as fuck to everycunt, saying some of the worst fucking things I could think of, all arrogant with it, laughing. And at other times I'd just generally leave Lynn to go home by herself on nights out while I went away with strangers to keep on drinking till the next day.

There were lots of low points. I was fucking up my relationship, fucking up my work, and I didn't give a fuck. In fact, I remember thinking to myself, 'If she ever asks me to pick between the booze and her, or if Donnie ever asks, or if anybody ever asks, I'll pick the booze.' And I fucking meant it. I didn't have that thought while I was drunk. I thought it when I was sober, during a weekday.

Does that make me an alky?

I feel like a fraud when I say I'm an alcoholic, because I was never having whisky in my cornflakes or anything, but I was ready to chuck everything away for the drink. I don't know if that makes me an official alky, but whatever I was, I stopped.

I stopped when I hit my actual, genuine low point.

Stopping Being an Alky

I was 29 when I stopped drinking. I stopped drinking on Monday 7th June 2004, and I haven't had a drink since.

It started with a weekend bender. It probably started on the Friday night, but it's the Saturday that I remember first. I don't know what I did on the Friday, but I'd definitely have been drinking. There's no way I wasn't drinking. Saturday was the big one, though. I remember that.

On the Saturday, me and Lynn were going to see a band at Nice N Sleazy, a band that some of her pals were in, and we were going with all these other pals of hers. I knew them all, and they were a good laugh, so I was looking forward to going there and getting wrecked. I wanted to get absolutely fucking wrecked.

When we were in there, I got a glass of Buckfast. They actually served Buckfast in Nice N Sleazy, in a glass. I've never liked Buckfast, but I got one, as well as a pint. I thought it was kind of naughty. I was hiding it behind my back, so that Lynn didn't see, because she wouldn't have approved. That's how I saw her, as a disapproving nag, despite all the shite I'd put her through. I'll have a cheeky glass of Buckfast and she won't know a thing. I thought I was being all sly, and I was showing off to one or two of the guys there. Don't tell the wife, lads!

I watched the band, and got drink after drink. I got wrecked, as planned.

All of us left, and there was talk of a party or something like that. We queued up at a cash machine, along with all these other people up the toon. Lynn was waiting in the queue, and some guy skipped in front of her. Lynn said something, and the guy just smiled and shrugged, as if to say, 'Tough. What are you going to do about it?'

I spat on him.

I stepped in, I said, 'Get fucking back, ya cunt,' and spat right at him. I don't think I spat right in his face, but towards his body. I don't think I've ever spat on anybody before. I was out of fucking control. I felt that this guy deserved the most vile fucking treatment going, and I wanted to be vile. I wanted to be a monster. The guy looked scared, and he went to the back of the queue. He looked like he thought he was going to get stabbed, and I liked it. If I was sober I would have felt nervous about a confrontation, I would have shat it and then regretted it later. But because I was drunk I just spat at the cunt, and that was it. I was an animal.

The next thing I remember is that I was at some party, with Lynn's pals, but Lynn wasn't there. She'd headed home. This party was at somebody's house – it was a family thing, with mums and dads, as well as folk my age. I was asking folk what this fucking thing was, just kind of ridiculing it. I think we were asked to leave, or I was asked to leave and some folk came with me. But before I left, I stole a bottle of vodka. It was like a litre of vodka, bigger than just the normal size. When I got outside, I was gloating about it, laughing at how I'd knocked their fucking vodka.

We headed back to a guy's flat, one of Lynn's pals. We had a few drinks, then I stayed there for the night. When I woke up on the Sunday, I was ready to do it all over again. It was lovely weather, so I arranged to meet up with Lynn's pals for some afternoon drinks, but first I headed home to get changed.

Lynn locked me out the house, and told me to stay away.

I was happy. I was happy to do that, because then she wouldn't be there, telling me to watch my drinking or telling me to watch my behaviour. I could do what I fucking wanted. Yeeha.

I met up with Lynn's pals and we started drinking again. We started drinking in the afternoon and kept it up until late at night. I was texting Lynn to see if she wanted to come out, but it was just to cover my arse; I just wanted to appear to want her out so that I didn't get criticised for not asking. I didn't want her out; she'd see the state of me and she'd try to make me stop.

By the end of the night I'd drunk myself sober, then drunk myself drunk again. I was trying to persuade Lynn's pals to go to a club, so I could keep drinking. I had work the next day, but I didn't care. I just didn't want to stop. I was almost falling asleep sitting up. There was a deep, warm tiredness in me. I wanted to stay out, but nobody was up for it, so I just headed home.

When I got there, Lynn was sleeping. And I went to bed beside her. I knew that I'd be in a bit of trouble the next day, but that would be fine. We'd been there before.

I woke up on Monday morning and checked the time. It was at some point after 10 a.m., and I was late for work. But I knew I wasn't going in. No way. I felt fucking bad.

I could hear Lynn working in our wee home office next door.

I felt that creeping feeling. That guilty feeling. I had behaved fucking terribly. I'd basically binned Lynn over the weekend in favour of the drink. I'd binned her, and went out with her mates, having a laugh and getting wrecked, while she sat in the house. And now I was in the house with her. Just me and her.

I'd ruined everything.

And then there was Donnie, in work. He'd be in there alone, carrying the company, doing everything himself. He was already on the verge with me. He'd already said he was thinking of chucking it. And here I was again.

I phoned him. He answered, and I told him I was sorry but I'd been on a bender and I couldn't come in, and that I'd make it up to him. He said it was fine and he'd see me the next day. Poor fucking guy.

I got up and opened the door to the wee office. Lynn turned around, and I said, 'Lynn, I'm sorry.' She looked disgusted when she saw my face, and turned back around to her computer. She almost looked shocked, and I don't know if it was the state of my puffy face, or what. But she looked disgusted. So I left the room.

I had to get out the house, I don't know why. It was maybe the fear of Lynn saying something, or maybe I felt like I didn't belong there. But I got ready, and left. I walked across the road to Glasgow Green and sat on a bench near the Clyde.

I looked over at the road at the front of Glasgow Green, at the people walking by on the pavement, and the folk driving by in their motors.

I just couldn't do it any more.

I just didn't see me as a part of it any more.

It's hard to put into words just how bad it felt. I can't even remember how deep this feeling was, but I remember thinking something, something that might sound a bit daft to you, but I thought, 'I don't have a name.'

That's meaningless when I write it here, it means fuck all. 'I don't have a name,' so fuck. It almost sounds like a good thing, like something to meditate on, to see yourself as non-existent or without a label or without baggage. It sounds liberating. But it wasn't like that. It was a feeling of not having any place here, and never having a place here. It wasn't an angry feeling, or a self-pitying 'poor me' feeling. It was a matter of fact. It was like being in a relationship that isn't working out, except it isn't a relationship with a person, it's a relationship with your life. You know it's over. You've fought for years to try and keep it together, but now you know it's over. It's fucking sad, but you don't want to fight for it any more, because you know it's over.

I was going to jump in the Clyde.

I thought about it. I was going to go along to the suspension bridge, about a ten-minute walk away, and jump in. It isn't a high bridge, you wouldn't break any bones when you hit the water, but I just wanted to drown. I wanted it to be cold and punishing. I almost wanted to regret it when the cold hit me, when it was too late. I wanted to die, but I also wanted it to be a punishment.

It became clear in my mind.

I started to feel a calm certainty.

I sat there calmly, knowing I was going to do it.

All it would take was a nudge. Just a wee nudge to get me to physically stand up and walk there.

It was almost like when I'm thinking of going for a haircut. It was that same feeling of knowing that I've got to, but something's holding me back. I just need to give myself that wee nudge, that wee feeling of 'Right, c'mon,' that wee nudge that comes from nowhere. I was waiting for that nudge.

As I was waiting, I thought about what would come next, what would come after I died.

Somebody would spot my body and phone the police or an ambulance. I'd be dragged out, and they'd have a look in my wallet and see my cards, and identify me. They'd find out my address, and they'd send a couple of officers round. Lynn would hear the buzzer on the door going, and she'd get up from her computer and wonder who it was, if it was maybe me. But it would be the police. They'd ask if they could come in, and they'd sit down in the living room and tell her that they'd found a body in the Clyde, and they have reason to believe it's me.

I imagined how she'd feel.

She just saw me half an hour ago, and now I was a body. I was gone.

I didn't think it in a self-important way, like how devastated everybody would be to lose somebody as special as me. It just felt fucking sad. Lynn would be in the flat, and there would be the things that belonged to me, my clothes in the wardrobe or a letter addressed to me, but I wasn't there any more. None of it was needed, and she'd have to chuck it out. It reminded me of how I felt after my mum died, when I saw that receipt in her purse.

I felt like I was grieving, but for myself. It was like I missed me and I wanted me back.

And that was it. That's what stopped me.

Something awakened.

I didn't want to die. I didn't want to fucking die.

I wanted to live.

I felt something like adrenaline go through me. A surge of energy, or clarity.

Everything became clearer, everything I saw and heard became focused. It was like getting back with somebody that you'd broken up with, somebody that you'd taken for granted, but now you realise how much you miss them and how much you love them, and you're looking at their face and smelling their hair and you'd do absolutely anything to not let it slide again, you'd do absolutely anything.

And I decided, right, that's it. It's over. No more. No more booze. No more. Not one more. Not one.

I couldn't come back here. I couldn't come fucking back here, to this place in my mind, to this place in my life. I needed to fucking know that I was never going to feel this way again. I couldn't take it any more. I couldn't take it. Please, please tell me I'm never coming back.

And I thought, 'Don't worry, you're not. It's over. It's over. Not one more. Not a shandy, not a soft drink between pints, none of that stuff you tried before. You're not "calming it a bit", you're not "watching it for a while", you're not cutting it out during the week but treating yourself at the weekend, you're not sticking to pints but staying away from wine, you're not sticking to wine but staying away from spirits, you're not doing any of that. One drink, and you're back here.'

It's over, mate.

It's over.

And with that, it was over. I was happy. It was still the worst hangover of my life, but there was light at the end of the tunnel. I could see it. There it fucking was.

It was over. I was so full of fucking hope. I was born again. Born again.

I went home and told Lynn the good news.
Naturally, she didn't believe me. Nobody did.
If I was them, I wouldn't have either.

No Longer an Alky

After the day I stopped drinking, I had a hangover that must have lasted for a month. It wasn't a normal hangover – my head wasn't sore, I didn't feel panicky, I didn't have the fear. But I had this timid way to me. It lasted far longer than what you could give the alcohol credit for. It was like I was shaken by what happened down at the Clydeside. It was like a hangover-hangover. An aftershock. It was like fucking PTSD or something.

I had a meeting to go to, with Soma Records. They wanted me to do a wee promo video for Slam, for their new single 'This World'. I went to meet them myself, because it wasn't to do with my company, it was more of a homer. We chatted about what they were after and the idea that I had, and I remember having that timid feeling. I remember feeling scared that they'd propose something that I wouldn't like, like an idea that wasn't up my street or something that was a huge amount of work for not enough money, because I didn't feel up to saying no. I just felt vulnerable as fuck, like anybody could ask me to do anything, and I'd do it. But luckily it was fine.

After a few weeks that timid feeling wore off, and it was replaced with this feeling of invincibility.

I felt invincible, because I really had stopped drinking. I could feel it in me. I'd actually fucking done it. Obviously, there was a chance of a relapse and everything, there always is, but the feeling that I'd conquered it felt so certain. It didn't feel like I'd beaten it for a while, it felt like I'd vanquished it. I felt like I'd won. The biggest fucking thing getting in my way, the biggest thing in my life, the biggest problem and the biggest interest in my life for years, was gone. And it was all because of me. I was in total control of my mind, and if you're in control of your mind, that's it, there's nothing else. I did it. And if I could do that, I could do fucking anything.

What I did next was I started doing lots of washing. I started putting lots of washing in the washing machine.

There were all these wee things I didn't usually bother doing around the house, because I was too busy drinking wine in bed. But now that I wasn't drinking I was bored out of my fucking mind. I started washing clothes all the time. Lynn seemed happy with that, and I was happy.

Honestly, I was bored out my mind.

I didn't go out that much any more.

Before, me and Lynn would normally go out over the weekend, have a few daytime drinks on the Sunday, have a laugh. But now I was getting fidgety. Now I was in a pub, and not really interested in being there. I'd rather be in the house.

The week after I stopped drinking there was something in the Botanic Gardens, some free Belle and Sebastian concert. We went along to that. The place was busy with people having drinks and smiling and enjoying the weather. But for me, there was just no point to me being there. Lynn asked if I was having a good time, and I said no, not really. She said I was being a downer, and I said, well, you fucking try coming to something like this when you're sober. When I said that, there was a flicker of understanding on her face. She wasn't happy about it, but I'm sure she understood. Most drinkers would.

Everything revolved around drinking. Without a drink, everything was shite. Everything was boring and pointless. I wasn't moany about it. It didn't make me sad. It just felt honest. This was how things were – a lot of things aren't that good, and it's one of the reasons why people get drunk.

A month or so later, we went to a wedding reception. Boring as fuck.

Boring beyond belief.

While I was there I bumped into the folk I was with on that last night of drinking. They couldn't believe I'd stopped drinking. They kept asking me how long I was stopping for, and I said forever, that's me out. They kept wanting me to have a drink. I told them I was about to top myself with that last hangover, that I couldn't drink again. And they were like, 'Fuck sake, have *one*.'

At a later date, I told my dad that I stopped, and that was pretty much his reaction as well. He said, 'I don't know if you want to go and do that.' This is a guy whose own brother topped himself because of alcoholism. And here's me, his son, telling him I was about to top myself for the same reason, therefore I'm never drinking again. 'Och, I don't know,' he said. 'It's a bit extreme.'

I was so bored. So, so fidgety. I wanted to do things. Do things, make things, do fucking anything. It wasn't to get away from the temptation of drinking, because I wasn't tempted. It was out of boredom. So fucking bored.

It was coming up for my 30th birthday, and Lynn asked me what I fancied doing, if I fancied a holiday. I told her that I couldn't go on the usual holiday, where I was sitting in a pub all day drinking pints and watching *Only Fools and Horses*. I'd go out my mind if I had to do that sober. I needed somewhere with things to do, lots of stuff. So she booked us a holiday to Disney World in Florida. Which was fucking perfect.

But even that got a bit boring.

When I got back, I made that video for 'This World' by Slam. In it, you'll see that my hair is all short and my face looks skinny. I lost lots of weight after I stopped drinking, and the reason my hair is so short is because I shaved it all off before I went to Florida. It was partly because I felt like I was going bald, and partly out of boredom.

A couple of months later was Hogmanay, my first sober Hogmanay since I was about 14. We went to a pub with a few pals. The bells rang, Happy New Year. It didn't mean anything to me. I wasn't in a downer, but it just felt like a Wednesday in the middle of March.

In the new year, Lynn mentioned that she wanted to go travelling. She'd been saying it for a while, but when I was drinking I would always say I couldn't. I was always negative. Always with worries and a reason to not go. How could I leave my company? How could I leave Donnie? How could I leave for a whole year? What would I do when I got back? Would I do free-lance stuff? What if it didn't work out? What if I was skint like before? I don't think I could handle that stress again. Would I go back to my old company, but as an employee? How would it all work out? How much would it cost? Could we not maybe do it a few years later?

Negative, negative, sitting in bed with my bottle of wine.

But when she asked this time, I was like: 'Aye. Fuck it. Fuck it, let's go.'

Comedy

Limmy.com DVD

Before me and Lynn went travelling in 2005, I made something called the Limmy.com DVD, which was a collection of all my videos from Limmy.com. I made 100 of them, and sold them from my site, which raised about the same amount of money as my round-the-world ticket.

I've not actually said anything about the videos on my site, have I? I've been so busy talking about boozing and losing the plot that I didn't mention all the good things I was getting up to. That's the demon drink for you. It's making me all negative and neglectful just typing about it.

I started putting wee videos on Limmy.com in 2002, after buying myself a video camera for my 28th birthday. I didn't really know what I wanted it for – maybe to just stick wee videos of me in my Flash things. I wasn't planning on making sketches. But on the night that I bought it I made up a quick wee video for Lynn. She was in her room, doing her freelance work, and she was getting a bit stressed out with having to work late. So I said to her that I'd make her a video in the living room, and she could come through to watch it when it was finished, for a wee break in her work. It was never made for anybody else to see.

I had this birthday card that Lynn got me, with the boyband Blue on it, because I was kind of into them at the time – in a jokey way. So I thought, right, I'll do a wee video where I'm this guy who's showing his mate this birthday card he got, and he's all happy because it's from Blue. But the mate (also played by me) is pointing out to him, well, it's not actually from Blue, don't be daft, he didn't actually get it from Blue. And then there would be some sort of argument. I didn't know what, I'd just make it up as I went along.

So I put the camera on the tripod, with the remote for the camera in my hand, and I recorded the thing, just pausing and unpausing as I switched positions between these two guys. The guy who insists he got the card from Blue ends up looking at the camera, smiling, and says, 'I'm freaking it, by the way. I'm freaking oot, by the way,' which was a good enough ending for me. Then I did this wee bit after it, as myself, saying to Lynn that I hope she enjoyed the 'play' and enjoyed her break. It's there on YouTube right now, if you fancy watching it.

I showed it to Lynn, and she thought it was funny. I liked it as well. It was daft, so I decided to stick it on my website. And I called it 'The Birthday Card'.

People started sharing it about, and I was all pleased that they liked it. So I wanted to make more.

Guy Fawkes was just around the corner, so I made up something for our company, a kind of funny viral video. There were three videos, and the general idea is that I'm handed a banger, one of those fireworks that just goes bang, but I think it's something else, something less harmful, like a sparkler, or a fag, or a lollipop, even though it's obviously a fizzing banger – then the thing goes off in my face. It doesn't sound that funny when I put it into words, but it's on YouTube as well, if you want to judge for yourself.

Anyway, that started getting sent all over the place. This was before YouTube and smartphones, but some guy had recorded a wobbly video of it off his computer monitor, and started sending it to his mates as an MMS. Then those mates sent it to their friends and family. And so on, in that good old-fashioned viral way. Until I was getting shown it by people that I knew, who'd got sent it by their auntie and folk like that.

The occasional person said hello to me in a pub, after recognising me. Now, that felt like the beginnings of fame, that. It was one thing for my website to be well known in the Flash community, but another to be stopped in the street by strangers.

I liked it, so I kept making more videos, until I ended up with this wee bundle. I had no intention of getting on the telly or anything like that. A stranger once said, 'You should be on the telly,' and I said, 'Haha, aye,' but I didn't give it a second thought.

Even when I was making the DVD, I didn't even consider it. I wouldn't know how to go about something like that, who to speak to, how it all begins. Not a clue. So it was pointless to consider.

But I made a professional effort with the thing, the DVD. I learned how to author it all, using this thing called Adobe Encore. I made a wee video menu, where I was sitting in a seat, telling the viewer to pick one of the videos on offer. I made wee video extras, I did an audio commentary, like these director's commentaries you get. I got the disc printed with me sitting on that seat, and the same picture printed on brown paper for the cover. I got 100 of them made, and sold the lot to the people who were on my blog, and sent them all out.

As I said, it managed to raise the same amount as the price of the plane tickets, but we'd already bought them. And I got money after selling my shares to Donnie, so that he had all of the company. That was me out. I was worried how Donnie would cope without me, but he ended up growing the company from one person to about fifteen. That's how much of a negative fucking energy I was.

But no more. No more negativity from me! I was away to travel the world!

We were going to Japan, Thailand, Australia, America, with a few countries in between. I couldn't fucking wait. Glasgow was grey and wet, grey skies, grey ground, grey buildings, grey everything. I had a picture of Thailand as my wallpaper on my computer, with its blue sky and blue sea and white sandy beaches and palm trees. Couldn't wait. I'd be away for a whole year. I imagined never coming back, I imagined finding some island and just living there. But more realistically, I imagined meeting all these fellow travellers, people like me who wanted to get away and explore and meet new people and, oh, I couldn't wait.

As it turned out, I fucking hated it.

No, I'm exaggerating. But the disillusionment hit me on the very first day. Our first place was Tokyo, and Jesus Christ, the people in that hostel, the westerners, you've never met a more anti-social bunch in your life. Nobody looked at anybody. It was like being on the underground. Fair enough on the underground – you've got no interest in striking up conversations on the underground, but you'd think it would be different in a hostel. I remember saying hello to some lassie as I walked past, and she pure looked away. I thought it was maybe because she thought I was coming on to her, but then Lynn did it later and the lassie just looked right through her. Maybe she was shy or something. But then it would happen somewhere else, not all the time, but enough to piss you off. I'm not talking about people who are depressed and want time alone, I'm talking about people who were otherwise smiley. Guys, lassies. You pass them in a corridor, you give them a smile or nod out of politeness, and you get fuck all back. It's almost infectious. You end up turning into them. Then somebody smiles and nods at you, and you're unprepared for it.

Then there were just irritating people. Cunts farting right in front of you in the dorm room. Cunts putting their absolutely stinking bare feet on a seat right next you. Cunts knocking the milk that you put in the fridge. Cunts coming into your room at 3 a.m., knowing that everybody is sleeping, but talking loud as fuck like it's 3 in the afternoon.

Then there's just general boredom. I got bored of seeing things. By the time we got to New York, which was our last stop, we couldn't be fucked going up the Empire State Building or over to the Statue of Liberty or anything. We ended up coming home to Scotland two months early. That's how much we'd had enough.

I was glad we went travelling, though. If I hadn't, I'd always be wondering what was out there. But now I know. There's fuck all.

I liked Las Vegas, though.

And LA.

And I loved Sydney.

One night near the end of our time in Sydney, which I think was in April 2006, I checked my email, and I had an email from the Comedy Unit.

I recognised the name. They were a production company, the folk who made these comedies that were well known in Scotland, like *Rab C. Nesbitt* and the sketch show *Chewin' the Fat*.

Somebody emailed me to say that one of my Limmy.com DVDs had landed on her desk. She really liked it, and she wanted to know who I was and if I wanted to do any comedy stuff with them.

I was like that to Lynn, 'Lynn! Look at this. Look!'

Lynn said, 'This is it!'

She suggested that we should head home to Glasgow. As in cut our travels short, about six months early. She said it was too good an opportunity to miss.

I said, 'Naw, fuck that.' I emailed the Comedy Unit to ask if they could wait, and they said they could wait.

Limmy's World of Glasgow

The email came at a very good time. You know how I said I hadn't seriously considered getting on the telly? Well, just after we started travelling, Lynn suggested I should, and that I should use all this spare time to write something, either a telly programme or just something to get noticed. So I did. I didn't really know what to make, though. I was considering making an animation, until I heard *The Ricky Gervais Show*. A podcast, the number one podcast in the world, and I thought it was hilarious. It was inspiring as well, because I realised that making something like that would be easy, much easier than an animation, because it was just audio. So I thought, 'Right, fuck it, I'm doing that.'

I wasn't sure what I wanted the podcast to be, exactly, I wasn't thinking about it that much, until that email from the Comedy Unit. That gave me a kick up the arse. I thought ahead to the meeting, which would be six months away when I finally got back home. I imagined them asking, 'So, Brian, do you have any ideas?' and me being put on the spot and having fuck all, and them saying, 'Bye bye.' Unless, of course, I had a big pile of ideas that I'd made earlier. And that big pile of ideas could be in the form of this podcast.

I got myself a wee notepad, and I kept my mind open for ideas.

I'd see things, I'd hear things, I'd remember things from the past, I'd do wee funny voices. I did a lot of funny voices. I'd been doing wee funny voices for ages, wee characters that I'd do when Lynn was about, or sometimes by myself. I'd put on a voice and go into character and ramble on for a while. Lynn would say,

'Oh, you've got to do something with that.' She loved that programme *Talking Heads*, the Alan Bennett one, and she said something like that would be good, with these characters just telling their stories. I hadn't watched it, really, but I got the gist of it, and I liked the idea.

So I started coming up with these characters. People have asked me how I came up with my characters, and it's a mixture of things.

Sometimes the characters came about because I had the voice first. For example, I'd do impressions of this guy me and Lynn knew. He had this dead low voice, kind of mumbly like Sylvester Stallone. My voice sounded a bit like that when I woke up in the morning, so I'd do the voice in bed when Lynn was wanting me to get up. I'd do this kind of layabout character that would talk about how much he just loved lying in his scratcher, lying in his pit, in his own dirt, week in, week out. It reminded me of that time I moved in with my mate, where I did pretty much nothing for a whole year. I thought about how it melted my brain, like that thing with the poster of the sunflowers, or all these wee other things I used to think. I put it all together, the voice and the layabout stuff and the insanity, and out popped Dee Dee. I gave him that name because of a guy I remembered from Carnwadric who had that nickname. He was nothing like Dee Dee, but I always thought the name was funny.

With other characters, it would be a mix of people I'd met in the past, or people I'd overheard, or the character would maybe be a side of my own character, like the gay side of me, or the violent side of me, or the side that was para about people looking down their nose at me.

I came up with nine characters, and I made a note of wee stories that would go well with them, just a sentence or two. Or I'd have an idea for a story first, then match it with a character. The ideas for stories would pop into my mind just by seeing things, glimpsing things, overhearing things, thinking things, remembering things from long ago, imagining things, imagining if this happened or that happened.

By the time I got home I had the idea for the whole thing. Not just the characters and stories, but the format as well.

I'd do an episode a day, a story a day, for twelve weeks, with each story being from a different character than the one before. It would be a lot of work, a lot of pressure, but I wanted to keep people's attention. I wanted them to look forward to that new episode every day. In a way, it was less pressure doing it daily, because if I did a shite episode, well, there would be a new one tomorrow. I wanted my subscribers to stick around. I didn't want them to fuck off and unsubscribe. I wanted to be on that iTunes chart. I wanted to be able to boast that I had a Top 10 iTunes podcast hit, to whoever I needed to boast to. I wanted to have lots of ideas. I wanted to have a good time and push myself and have something to show for it. The whole exercise was partly creative, and partly marketing.

With that plan in mind, I started making the episodes.

I set up a small home studio. When I say 'home studio', I mean I had a mic plugged into a computer, a mattress against the wall to dampen the room reverb, and a pair of tights over a wire coathanger for a pop filter.

Before recording each episode, I'd look at my notes. They weren't much. As an example, take the one where Dee Dee gets the bus to Yoker. You might know it as a sketch in *Limmy's Show* (if you don't, it's on YouTube), but it was an episode in my podcast first.

I got the idea from back in my younger years, when I'd go on my adventures up the toon. While up there, I'd see this bus going to a place called Yoker. I thought it was a strange-sounding place, and I wanted to go and find out what it was like. I wanted to use my bus pass to go there and get off and have a wander, then get back on. But I always had the fear that I wouldn't be able to get back on, due to my bus pass not covering that zone. Then I'd be stranded in Yoker. And the locals would be wondering, 'Who's this we have here?'

That sounded like something this Dee Dee character would get up to, so I made it one of his stories. I improvised it all, but first I wrote a wee bullet-point list of things that I wanted to happen. I wanted to know what the beginning, middle and end were, roughly, before I hit record. Then I'd hit record and ramble on and on and on. That episode ended up being about 20 minutes long, but I recorded about twice that, and edited it down.

I did that for each episode, and I recorded about 20 episodes before I launched the podcast, a wee stockpile in case I couldn't record any new episodes on certain days. Then I made up a wee logo, and I made up a wee page on Limmy.com to introduce the characters. I did all that because I read that you had a better chance of being featured by iTunes if you made all that effort.

I told everybody on my blog that I'd be launching the podcast in a few weeks, so they should get subscribed now in advance, and they should tell all their friends and family to do the same.

Then I finally launched the thing.

And I checked the charts. Daily. Hourly. Every ten minutes.

I watched it appear on the Top 100, and that was fucking exciting. There it was. Number 98 or whatever.

Then it was up to 40.

Then it went up and up like that.

But I wanted it on that Top 10 chart that was at the side of iTunes. That's where I fucking wanted it.

Then, one morning, I checked iTunes, and there in the Featured window, slap bang in the middle of the main iTunes podcast page, was the big fucking logo for Limmy's World of Glasgow. What a fucking buzz that was.

Then I looked at the chart. I was something like number 4 in the UK comedy chart, and in the Top 10 for all UK podcasts, comedy or otherwise. I was the only homemade cunt in there. Everything else was by the BBC or Comedy Central or something like that.

The papers took an interest. They did an interview (it was the *Sun*, please forgive me) and they sent a photographer round and all that. It was fucking superb. It was just what I wanted. I don't mean being in the *Sun*. I mean for me to get in the charts and get some attention, and then somehow use that attention (and the stuff that I'd made) as proof that I should maybe be on the telly or something.

I'd postponed meeting the Comedy Unit up until that point, but now I was ready to see them. Now that I was an iTunes UK Top 10 podcast smash. A bigshot.

Stand-up

The folk in the Comedy Unit were a pleasure to meet. They were upbeat and happy to see me. They asked me what I fancied doing, what I was aiming for. I said that I was sort of maybe thinking of maybe somehow possibly having some kind of sketch show or something. It was hard to just come right out with it, because I was expecting to get laughed out of the place. After all, who the fuck was I? I was just some guy from the internet. A newcomer. And a 32-year-old newcomer at that. Practically a has-been.

But they said they'd be happy to work with me on that, to try and develop something, but warned me that it takes a long time. So I left it with them.

In the meantime I got an email from a guy asking me if I wanted to do a live show for the Glasgow Comedy Festival, coming up the following year in March 2007. Just a wee one, a one-hour show. He said he liked my podcast and he saw me in the paper, and he was in the business of organising shows. He'd book the venue and organise the tickets and all of that.

I replied right away to say no.

Fuck that.

I'd never done stand-up before. I'd never done any kind of performance thing before. No school plays, no karaokes, nothing. And as much as I like an audience amongst a group of pals, the idea of getting up in front of an audience-audience, no, fuck that.

I told Lynn about it. I almost didn't want to tell her, because I knew she'd try to persuade me to say yes. I told her, though. And, as expected, she persuaded me to say yes. She just fucking bombarded me.

So I said alright. Fucking hell, alright.

What a fucking insane thing to do, to agree to do a stand-up show, when you've never done it before. Insane.

I had until March, and this was about October/ November. I had about three or four months to write a one-hour show. But more importantly, I had till then to get used to being in front of an audience. I didn't want my show to be the first time in front of an audience. I'd fucking crumble and cunts would be wanting their money back.

I decided to do a wee spot at The Stand in Glasgow. The Comedy Unit did a comedy night there every month called 'Rough Cuts', where they'd showed some of my videos after we had our meeting. I asked them if I could do a wee bit of stand-up as well, just to get some experience, and they said aye.

I just want you to know, every step here terrified me. Firstly, being asked to do the show. Then me agreeing to it. Then me asking to do a wee spot at The Stand, and them agreeing to it. Every wee step made me think, 'What the fuck am I doing?'

But I'd agreed to do it, so that was that. All I had to do was break myself in with this first wee spot. And all I had to do before that was try and think of what the fuck this wee spot was going to be.

I didn't want to do normal stand-up, normal observational stand-up. That wasn't what I was into. I was into sketches, and weird things. So I came up with the idea of doing a sketch. I'd do a one-man sketch, where I'd play both characters by turning to the left and right; that's what I was kind of known for with my Limmy.com videos, like that 'Birthday Card' one. So I wrote this sketch called 'Brother John', a kind of *Twilight Zone* thing. A guy arrives at a pub to meet his mate, and he happens to ask if his mate's brother will be coming out later. The mate doesn't know what the guy's talking about. He doesn't have a brother. They have an argument over it, one that spans decades, with both of them accusing the other one of being on the wind-up. The guy eventually accepts that his mate doesn't have a brother, that it was all in his mind. But then, one day, the mate says that his brother is coming out for a drink. The guy doesn't understand. The mate had been saying he didn't have a brother, for decades. Then I tell the audience that the guy sees this brother from a distance, coming into the pub. The guy can't believe his eyes, because do you know who this brother was?

Then I point to somebody in the audience, and shout 'Youuuuuu!' Then I say thanks, you've been a great audience, and walk off. And that whole sketch lasts for almost ten minutes.

It was quite a weird and anti-climactic thing to do, but that sort of thing is right up my street. Plus the good thing about doing something weird is that you can hide behind the weirdness. If you're scared of not being funny, it gives you a protective shield of weirdness. It would be one less thing to think about, because all I wanted to do was just get on stage, do something without making a cunt of it, then get off. Simple as that.

So I rehearsed and rehearsed and rehearsed.

I'd never rehearsed lines before. I'd never had to remember the words to something for that long, word for word, all the movements, no mistakes, no ums or ems. But I rehearsed and rehearsed and rehearsed. I rehearsed in the house, in the shower, on my bike. I rehearsed in bed, thinking about it in my head. I started to rehearse it at twice the speed, I knew it that well. That's when I really became confident, when I could do it fast as fuck. I started looking forward to the big night. I wasn't too worried about it not being funny, I just didn't want to fuck it up and have a fucking panic attack and run off the stage. But I felt good. I knew it back to front.

Then, one day, while I was rehearsing in the bedroom, I happened to look at myself in the mirror while I was saying my lines. I made eye contact with myself. And it broke my concentration. Just by looking at my eyes, it distracted me from my lines, and I couldn't remember my place.

I looked away and restarted my lines, then made eye contact with myself again as a test, to see if it was a one-off. But it broke my concentration again.

I thought, 'Oh no.'

It was the same way that I sometimes can't concentrate on what somebody's saying if I'm looking at their face or their eyes. I sometimes have to look away.

I thought, 'You're fucked. If you happen to look at somebody's eyes, you're fucked. You need to get on top of this, or you're fucked.'

So I kept looking at myself when I was rehearsing. I looked at myself from the side, straight on, on the move, standing still. I looked away, looked back. Kept doing it until it didn't affect my concentration any more.

That's it, I was fine. I was looking forward to it again.

Then, one night, I went to the toilet, and I thought I'd rehearse while I was there. The light was off, so it was pitch black. I started saying my lines, and I noticed I couldn't do it. It was something to do with the dark. I was used to moving my eyes around and seeing things, and now there was nothing. It was distracting. I was too aware of myself or something.

I thought, 'You're fucked. It'll be dark in The Stand. They have the lights off in the audience, and all you'll see is darkness, especially with the lights in your face.

The problem now isn't that you'll make eye contact, it's that you won't make eye contact. You're fucked.'

So I kept rehearsing in the dark, over and over, until it wasn't a problem any more.

Rehearsed, rehearsed, rehearsed. Rehearsed with music on, rehearsed in silence, rehearsed with the telly on and people speaking over me. I tried to think of everything that would put me off, and I rehearsed in that situation, until I felt good.

Then came the big night.

Earlier that day I felt alright. A wee bit nervous, but alright, because I'd rehearsed it a million times. As it got closer to when it was time to go round to The Stand, I started getting more nervous. Just some tingles in my belly.

When I was finally in the place, waiting to go on, I was absolutely shiting myself.

I'd brought along Lynn and a couple of folk I knew. We were sitting at a table down the front, waiting for the compère to come on. Lynn and the others were chatting amongst themselves, and sometimes to me. I wasn't listening. I was pretending to listen, smiling away and nodding, saying a few words back, pretending to be alright. I don't know if they saw through it, because my face felt like all the blood had drained away.

The place was filling up. I was looking at the audience, the folk who would be seeing me up there on stage. They weren't here to see me. None of them knew me. I was looking at their faces and trying to gauge if they were nice people.

I went to the toilet, just to rehearse again, in the cubicle. I got a few words in, then I made a mistake. I hadn't made a mistake in ages. It freaked me out. I'd rehearsed in every kind of environment, except the environment of shiting myself. Oh no. Oh fucking no.

I went back to my seat, and the compère came on. He told me beforehand that he'd do his routine for ten minutes or so, then introduce me, and I was to just get up and walk on the stage.

Was this really going to happen?

I was watching him do his thing, and watching people laughing. He was funnier that I was going to be. I was honestly fucking shiting it. Utterly shiting it. I knew that I'd be on that stage in ten minutes.

Then five minutes.

I felt fucking sick. I wasn't going to spew up, but I felt ill. I felt like I had the flu or something. My hands were shaking like fuck, my face felt all pale and tingly. My belly was tingling, my chest was all tight. And I was scared. So, so scared.

I have never been that scared in my life. Not before, not since. You remember me saying how scared I was back when I nearly got jailed, back when I was told that the judge might jail me, and I was picturing how I would cope in jail with all these bad people. Well, this was scarier. I'm not joking.

It's like a primal thing. A primal fear. A survival instinct. Without the approval of other people, you will be cast out of the city walls or the village or the cave that you live in, and without other people you're fucked. No food, no family, nothing. Humans don't have claws or big teeth or the strength of a bear. Humans have people, other people. Without other people, you're fucked. These people in the audience at The Stand are people. They are People. You fuck it up in front of them, it's over. You will die. You are about to die.

Eventually the compère finished, and said, 'Well everybody, enough from me. We've got a great night of comedy for you tonight, we've got new material, we've got some videos to show you, but first, and this is his first time on stage, so please give a warm welcome to Limmy!'

People clapped, and I felt myself stand up and walk towards the stage. I got up there, stood in front of the mic and started speaking. And I felt alright. Getting on the stage didn't make me feel worse, it made me feel better. I didn't have the time to worry, because I was too busy doing the sketch.

Everybody was quiet while I was doing it, which was what I expected. When I did the punchline, if you can call it that, the bit where I point at somebody and shout 'Youuuuu!', a few people laughed. Most people didn't. But one or two people thought it was hilarious.

Whether they thought it was hilariously funny or hilariously shite, it didn't matter. That's all I wanted, really. In fact, that sums up what I want with most of my comedy things. I'd rather a few people were pissing themselves, rather than everybody doing a mild chuckle.

I came off the stage and went back to my table, relieved as fuck. Lynn said well done, and so did the others I was with, then they went back to watching the rest of the show.

I was watching the other comedians, but I was thinking about the audience, how their attention had moved on from me to something else. Same with Lynn and the others. Everybody just moved on. I was no longer important, and it felt good to realise that. Nobody cared. There wasn't a big trial that followed my performance. I wasn't put in the dock and quizzed about why I had the cheek to think I deserved to be on that stage, or why I deserved to be a part of the human race.

Doing that first bit of stand-up, it broke something in me. To be so scared of doing something, so, so, so fucking scared, so fucking scared, but then to do it anyway, to choose to do it, to not be forced, but to choose to do it. It broke something in me. It changed something in me.

I did a few more wee appearances between then and my show. Five minutes here, five minutes there. I got an email from the tour manager for Jet, the Australian rock band, who liked my podcast. They wanted me to introduce them at the Academy in Glasgow. So I went along and met them, which was mental, and I did this thing. I pretended to the audience that Jet were stuck in traffic, so they had me instead, and I started singing 'Are You Gonna Be My Girl' for about ten seconds, in as annoying a way as I could. You had to fucking hear the boos I was getting, boos and shouting from about 2,500 people. It was brilliant.

So by the time I did my show a week after that, in front of about 120 people, I had no nerves at all. None. I did a few of my characters from *Limmy's World of Glasgow*, all these monologues, as well as the one-man sketches and some other stuff, and I showed some videos in between. It all went down well, and I had no nerves at all.

I was asked if I wanted to do a run at the Fringe, and I said aye, without hesitation.

So if you've ever thought about doing stand-up, but then you think, 'No, I couldn't do that, not me,' I am here today to say to you right now that you can.

Opportunities

I did my first Fringe later that year, in 2007, and it went well, I enjoyed it. It was in this wee 50-seater place called The Stand 2. It was the place where I saw the two guys from the dealer's flat, if you remember. I'd get the train through from Glasgow every day, do my show, then head back. It was like a holiday, really.

I called it 'Limmy's Show'. I knew that the Comedy Unit were still chatting with BBC Scotland about telly possibilities, so I wanted to do something that looked like it could be put on the telly, right down to the name of the show. I had video sketches, live sketches, monologues, just like my Glasgow Comedy Festival one, but all new. I hoped that some bigshots would come along and see the show, and maybe offer me something, in case the BBC thing didn't work out. And some did. A few production company folk would give me their card or give me an email after seeing the show.

When the Fringe run was finished, I got an email from some telly producer person, saying that they'd like to meet me. They liked the podcast and my stand-up, and they wanted me to get involved in some comedy programme they were making. They asked me if I'd be available to go through to Edinburgh for a chat about it, and I said aye. I didn't know what it was going to be about, but I said aye.

I got the train through, and there was somebody waiting for me at the station, to take me to the meeting. He wasn't the guy who emailed me, he was some other guy, and there was something about him that put me off. He looked a bit like a rat.

He didn't look shady, he didn't look dangerous or devious. He just looked like a rat, kind of nervy, and he didn't stand upright. Plus he had a scratch on his nose. That especially didn't give me a good feeling. I'm not some kind of professional cunt where everybody has to be standing bolt upright and everybody must take care of their nose, but right away there was a feeling of amateurishness about him, and about the whole thing.

He drove me to the front door of what looked like an upstairs bar. When we got in, the place was dead – no music, a few leather chairs, creaky floorboards, and this waiter in a fancy uniform. I was introduced to the guy who emailed me. He was a bit older than me. He looked a bit like Hannibal Lecter, Anthony Hopkins's one, but slightly younger. I shook the Hannibal guy's hand and I mentioned how the place was dead, and he said it was a private members' club. I thought, 'Oooh, a private members' club.' I'd never been in one before, and I wondered if this was where all the bigshots went.

We had a bit of small talk before I sat down. He said he really liked my podcast. He said, 'Yeah, it's really great.' So I said a bit about how I made it, kind of self-deprecating stuff, with a few wee jokes. He waited until I was finished, then he did this thing that put me off him a bit. He smiled and nodded, but his eyes weren't smiling. He nodded and smiled like that, and just repeated what he said before. He said, 'Yeah, it's really great.'

He really did seem like Hannibal Lecter then.

Anyway, we sat down and he turned his laptop towards me to show me what this was all about. I was shown a video of these puppets, but with people's heads superimposed over the puppets' heads, chatting away. It lasted about three minutes.

I didn't like it.

It was in its very early stages, but even at that, it was rough. It didn't look good, the patter was shite, there was no story, it wasn't a sketch or a snippet of a sitcom, it was just kind of fuck all. Keep in mind that I like weird stuff, I like stuff that isn't necessarily funny. But honestly, this was fuck all.

I did a few fake laughs through my nose here and there, just so the place wasn't silent.

When it was finished, I tried to give it a few compliments, then I said, 'But it's not really my cup of tea.'

He said that I shouldn't really judge it on that one video, because it was in its early stages, and if I didn't find any of it funny, well, that's why he'd like to get me involved. I could be in it, and write a bit.

I said, 'Och, it's really just not my cup of tea, the puppets thing,' and that I'd want to change things so much that I may as well do my own thing.

He kept at it, trying to be persuasive, and I started to feel my heart race a bit. I was somehow just going to have to say no, and leave, but I didn't know how. I could have done with Lynn being there.

But then he said something that made it pretty easy for me.

He said something along the lines of, 'You know, you've been given an opportunity here. Your podcast is great, it's got you lots of attention, but you need to capitalise on that by taking opportunities like this, otherwise it'll all just slip through your fingers.'

That made it easy for me. It made it easy to confront him. I don't like confrontations, but he patronised me, and sometimes when I get patronised, this hormone gets released into my bloodstream, and this hormone says to me, 'Are you taking that?'

I said, 'No, I don't agree with that, sorry. I mean, what you're saying, then, is that I've got to do this, or there might not be anything else for me. You're saying that this is it. It's kind of like scare tactics.'

He was like, 'No, not at all.'

And I was like, 'Well, I think it is. I think it is. You're trying to persuade me to do this by saying that this is my big opportunity and I won't get another one like it.' I pointed at the video and said, 'The fact is, I just don't think this is very good. I mean, that's the truth. D'you know what I mean? I just don't like it.'

I don't know if you think that was harsh or argumentative. But that was fuck all compared to what I felt like saying.

I felt like saying, 'I don't like your video, and I don't like you either, mate. You're a creepy bastard, with that way you smiled earlier without your eyes smiling. And what's with this rat cunt here? He hasn't said a word the whole time we've been here. It's like you've got him under your spell. It's like you're some sort of Dracula cunt, hiding away here in this creepy wee club, with your wee rat henchman, some poor guy that you turn into a rat. How did he get the scratch on his nose? Did you hit him? Or did he get it when he was in rat form? Is it from a mouse trap? Is there a wee hole in the skirting board here? Is that where he lives?'

But I didn't say that. I just said the thing about the video. I was fucking raging inside. I don't know why it pissed me off so much. Maybe it was the Jacqueline McCafferty side of me. It felt good to say it, it felt empowering. I felt like he had made a move to assert some kind of dominance over me, so I had to assert some dominance over him – by politely saying, in so many words, that his thing was shite.

The meeting finished soon after that, we shook hands and I got a lift back to the station from the rat.

I had a few other similar opportunities come my way, with the same kind of patter, and I knocked them all back. But I was starting to wonder if I really was going anywhere.

I decided to do another live show, for the Glasgow Comedy Festival in March 2008. But writing that show really got me wondering what I was doing and if it was all worth it. I ended up thinking about topping myself.

I announced I was doing three dates at Oran Mor, and they sold out right away, before I knew what I was going to do. I didn't want to do what I'd done before, with the character monologues. I wanted to just be myself on stage, but put the characters in video sketches. But I was worried that people wouldn't like it. But that's what I wanted to do. It was fucking getting to me. Plus I had 90 minutes to fill. This wasn't just a wee 60-minute show like the ones I'd done before. This was two 45-minute halves, and I didn't know how to fill them. I'd be thinking about what to do and what to write from when I woke up to when I went to sleep. I'd be in a trance all day, trying to make ideas come to me. Lynn would talk to me about other things, and I wouldn't be listening. We'd get into these arguments because I was being all distant, and that ended up making it harder to come up with anything. It's hard to come up with funny ideas when everything's falling apart. I had to come up with 90 minutes of stuff, and I couldn't fucking think.

I thought, right, fuck it, I can't do it.

I can't fucking do it.

I said to Lynn that I'm going to cancel the shows, because I can't fucking do it. It's killing me. I just wanted the whole thing to go away.

Lynn said I couldn't cancel the shows. She said if I cancelled the shows, 'You'll be finished,' in terms of my comedy career. The shows had already sold out, and to just chuck that away and say that I didn't have a show, it would make me look unreliable. Plus I was having these chats with the Comedy Unit about a possible sketch show, and it would make me look bad in terms of that.

I just didn't know what the fuck to do. So I just thought, right, here's what I'm going to do.

I'm going to cancel the shows. I'm going to cancel them, and tell everybody I'm sorry. And that'll be the end of my comedy career. Good. And then I'll break up with Lynn, because our relationship is on the rocks anyway. She's had enough, I'm a selfish cunt and I've stopped trying, and she'd be better off with somebody fresh and new. Then I'll have fuck-all money coming in, and my life won't be worth living with all the stress and the downers. I'll break up with her, and I'll get whatever money I can from the house. I'll go back to that time that was stress free, and I'll just hit the fucking bottle this time, just drink the money away, and when it's about to run out, I'll have one last giant drink and slash my wrists. Because fuck this. Fuck all of this.

All I had to do was make that first move, just send off that email to say the shows were cancelled, and that would set the wheels in motion. That would be it.

But I didn't do it.

I can't remember what stopped it, but it was probably the chat I had with Lynn. She sat me down and asked me what the problem was. She asked me what I'd written so far, what I was thinking, and I just went through it with her. This giant foggy problem in my head with no solution then became a bit more easy to get my head around. She helped me break it down into wee pieces. It became more manageable, it became easier to see. That relaxed me, it made ideas come easier, until I eventually put together a show.

All thanks to Lynn.

I don't want to make you cringe and say that Lynn is my rock or my anchor or anything like that. It would probably make her cringe as well. I'd say she's more like a god. It's like something out of the Bible. I cry for help and feel like giving up, but instead of receiving sympathy, I'm told that I'll be finished. A harsh truth. Followed by a period of being forsaken, or forsook. A period of self-pity. And then, when I'm broken, I receive mercy, and wisdom. I did the show in front of her in the kitchen, and she told me what to keep and what to bin. The show was far better because of her advice, and she likes to remind me. 'That show would have been shite if it wasn't for me,' she says now and then. And I tell her that she's right. I give praise and thanks. I sound fucking sarcastic, but I'm serious.

The show went down very well, and I had a cracking time doing it. My characters were in video sketches, and I was being myself on stage, smiling and having a laugh.

The Comedy Unit asked if they could come along on the Sunday show and film it, to show it to the commissioner at BBC Scotland, and I said aye.

The commissioner liked what he saw. I imagine seeing me in front of an audience must have helped. I wasn't just some guy with a handful of videos and a podcast where the episodes sometimes meandered on for 25 minutes. He could see that I could make these three-minute video sketches, with characters or animations, and I could also be myself in front of an audience and do these observational things or weird live sketches – and most importantly, the audience was laughing. Enough of them anyway.

The Comedy Unit gave me the good news. BBC Scotland wanted me to make a pilot for a sketch show.

Fucking brilliant.

Take that, Dracula cunt.

Limmy's Show Pilot

It was about April in 2008 that I got the news I was getting a pilot, by which point I'd already agreed to do the Fringe in August that year. I think if I'd got the news about the pilot first, I wouldn't have bothered with the Fringe. Live stuff can be unpleasant. There are nerves involved and there's the risk of forgetting your routine. But with videos it's all under your control.

I wasn't sure what I wanted to do with the pilot, what format. It was suggested to me that it could be a stand-up show filmed in front of an audience, or maybe even just bits of it filmed in front of an audience. But I said no, no, no. No thanks. I don't want to go back there. I just want my comfort zone, please. Just video, please. My comfort and joy.

I thought, right, what could I put in this? I thought of a few videos that I'd already made, ones that went down well at my live shows, plus a few non-video routines that I'd like to make sketches out of, and a few brand new things. But I wasn't sure about how to tie it all together. I was thinking of somehow making the end of one sketch flow into the beginning of another. I wanted to be really clever with it. Or the sketches could all be connected by me walking about Glasgow. I'd stop to talk to the camera to moan about something or make a point, then I'd walk away at the end, past some house. And in the house you'd see Dee Dee, that type of thing.

But it was suggested to me that it could be a pain in the arse to write something like that. Plus it could be impractical. What if one of the sketches didn't work out and I had to drop it? It would break the continuity. So I nodded and said aye, fuck it. But you can still see the remnants of the idea in the pilot. If you watch the John

Paul sketch near the start, I'm looking at his MySpace page at the beginning as Limmy, then I appear at the end as a passer-by. It doesn't make sense, but that's the sort of thing I like.

That John Paul sketch was the first one we filmed. And I was surprisingly nervous.

We'd decided to film that one first, because I wasn't in it for most of the sketch. It was Tom, one of the other actors. All he had to do was get chased about a park, with not many lines, and I appeared at the end. It would give me time to get used to things. Used to directing. Now there was something. Directing. Me, a director. Me, the ned. The criminal. The headbutter of shop shutters. I felt like an imposter when I was referred to as that. And I felt like an imposter when I turned up for that first day of filming.

I was driven to the Botanic Gardens, where we'd be filming, and there waiting were all the crew. There was this big van, with cables lying about, and a dozen crew members waiting for me.

The nerves hit me.

It only lasted a few seconds, but I shat it a bit, seeing all these people for the first time, these professionals, and me being driven towards them not entirely knowing what I'm doing. Plus there's the feeling that you can't back out. There are people here whose time has been paid for, and you can't walk away, and you can't just suddenly not know what you're doing.

The feeling passed. I'd already filmed this sketch before, it would be easy. And it was. It took an hour or so to film that particular sketch, and I got comfortable with chatting with everybody and asking the cameraman to film things this way or that. But as we moved on to the later sketches, things got a wee bit more difficult.

They didn't get more difficult for me, but I saw them get more difficult for other people. They started to seem stressed, and I thought it was because of me. I'd see the cameraman rubbing his head now and then and not looking as happy as he did when I first met him. The first assistant director was the same, putting his head in his hands and talking about running out of time. I had a feeling that I wasn't doing it properly. And I wasn't, really. As a director, you're supposed to turn up with a list of shots and talk it through with everybody quickly and get cracking. But at that stage in my career I was used to just having a lot of it in my head. So during the filming I was probably doing a lot of 'Em, right, let me think, so … no, actually, in fact, we need another shot of … em, let me think.'

I sometimes felt like I knew what I was talking about but I didn't know how to say it. And because I didn't know how to say it, I felt like I came across as clueless, and I started getting defensive about it. On one occasion there was a problem with filming a certain shot, so I had a think about it, then I decided in my head about what to do. But I could see some of the others talking about it, without me. The cameraman, the first assistant director and two of the producers, chatting amongst themselves, saying things like, 'Well, if we film it this way, we'd be able to …'

I shouted over and said, 'Here, it's fine, I'm just going to do it this way,' but one of them said, 'Sorry, Brian, just a second,' and they kept chatting.

I was fuming about that. In my head, I mean.

Then they came over and one of them said, 'Okay, what we're thinking …'

I pretended to not hear, and I said, 'Right, let me show you what I want.' And I told them what I wanted. It felt good. Even if I'd got the wrong end of the stick, it felt good.

We filmed all of the pilot in about a week, then I went in to the edit and the dub (the sound stuff) until it was all done and dusted. I liked how it all looked. I didn't like my hair, but I generally liked it all.

Me and Lynn watched it on the telly. We were both nervous, so we were sitting there on the couch, not laughing. Lynn was apologising for not laughing, saying she was just nervous. But I was thinking that she simply didn't find it funny.

I checked my blog to see what everybody thought of it. Most people said they liked it, with a lot of other folk saying they thought it was shite. Most of the people who said it was shite were anonymous, so I didn't know if they just had it in for me. As for the people who said they liked it, I didn't know if they were saying it to just be nice. I really had no idea how it went down. I felt a kind of nothingness. As much as I didn't want to do the live stuff again, at least with the live stuff you knew where you stood. People will laugh or they won't. You get the truth.

I wondered how it was going down with the commissioner.

Was I going to get a series?

How fucking humiliating it would be if I didn't get a series. There was a pilot for another sketch show on BBC Scotland a week later, called *Burnistoun*. I was pally with the guys who made it. People seemed to like that more – it had a laughter track and it just seemed more fun, whereas mine was weirder. I thought that BBC Scotland wouldn't commission two sketch shows, they'd just commission one, and *Burnistoun* was the safer bet. How fucking humiliating if that happened.

Then I got the news that both were getting a series. *Limmy's Show* was getting a series.

Thank fuck.

Six fucking episodes, plenty of work, and I'd be getting paid for it. No more stand-up. And I wouldn't have to go back to having a real job, not for a good while. I'd be able to just lie about doing fuck all, playing games and watching the telly.

Then Lynn said she wanted to have a baby.

The Last Time I Took Drugs

It was summer 2009. Before we tried to have a baby, we decided to head to Ibiza for our holiday. It was almost like one last bit of fun together. We were going to go to T in the Park the week after we got back, but first we'd go on this holiday to Ibiza, to celebrate the last of our youth. Not that we were planning anything that mental, mind you. We went to Figueritas, which was quite a quiet place compared to the Ibiza places we went to before, like San Antonio. When we got there it was relaxing, with families and slightly older people and generally less carry-on. We just sort of lazed about. But near the end of the holiday we decided we'd head over to San Antonio for old time's sake, because that was where we had our first holiday together. That's where all the clubs were. One last mad night before we tried to become a mum and dad, before I had to keep my insides clean.

We got the bus over, and I wondered where I was going to get a pill. I wasn't sure if I really wanted one, because the pills I'd been getting in Glasgow for the last few years hadn't been that brilliant. I thought it was maybe just me. Maybe my serotonin was all used up or something. I wasn't sure if I could be bothered getting my hopes up. But not long after getting off the bus I saw some young guys gubbing pills as they walked along the pavement. I heard their English accents, so I asked them where they got their pills. They pointed over to some guy down at the beach, a Spanish-looking guy.

I went over to the guy and asked him if he had any pills, and he gave me this pink one. I'd never had a pink one before, so I thought it was maybe a shiter. But I paid for it anyway. Then I gubbed it and we headed to Eden.

I think I was the oldest cunt in there.

The last time I was there was in 2001, when I was 26. Now I was 34. I felt a bit self-conscious, a bit of a dad, with my receding hairline and everything. I kept to the outskirts while I waited to come up on the pill, if I ever would come up. I was worried that I wouldn't, because then there would be fuck-all point in me being there. I'd have to put on this act to Lynn that I was enjoying myself in a club in Ibiza while being straight as a fucking die, otherwise her night would be fucked as well as mine.

But then I started to come up.

And then come up even more.

And then I felt fucking cracking.

It wasn't like one of those half-measure pills I'd been getting in Glasgow. It was a fucking cracker, this one. Best one I could remember. I had moved from the outskirts of the dancefloor to the middle, and I was shouting 'Yeeeeeha!'

I felt like I was back. I was saying that to Lynn, 'I'm fucking back!', telling her that it was the best pill I'd had in years. I was clapping away loud as fuck, that way that makes your hands sore. Every time the beat dropped, I was like 'HhhhhhyyyYAAAAAAAS!', and 'Fuckin YAAAAAAS!'

Younger cunts were looking at me, but they weren't looking in that 'Good on ye, mate' way that folk used to do when I was younger. They looked at me like I was a headbanger, like I was maybe a dangerous cunt. But I didn't care. I just kept saying to Lynn that it was the best night of my life for a long time, best night of my life, best night for a long time. I was kissing her and telling her I loved her, kissing her and telling her that that's me back. Telling her that I couldn't wait for T in the Park. Couldn't wait. Couldn't wait to get in that Slam Tent and do this all over again. Best night in ages, Lynn.

A week later, we were at T in the Park. I managed to get a pill, and I hoped it would be even half as good as the one I had in Ibiza. I gubbed it kind of early evening, I didn't want to gub it too late, because we were only there for the day and we'd be heading home on the bus at 11 p.m. or whenever it was.

I waited to come up, but after an hour I wasn't really getting anything.

Not long after that, I started to feel something. Except it didn't feel like an eccie. It felt like an acid. It felt like a mild acid. Like a half or quarter acid. And after about two hours it didn't get any better. It didn't make me feel like dancing.

I was like that, 'Oh fuck off.'

I tried to dance. I went to the Slam Tent and tried to get into it, but I couldn't.

Lynn asked me how I felt, and I said that the pill was fucking shite, I was just tripping.

What made it worse was that folk were coming up to me and wanting a picture. I'd been on the telly by that point, with the pilot for *Limmy's Show*, plus folk just recognised me from YouTube stuff. It just wasn't something I wanted at that time. I never let it show, though, I never said, 'No pictures, please,' or anything. But just imagine it. Imagine the para feeling you'd get on acid or whatever, then add to that the fact that people genuinely are turning their heads and staring at you. Strangers really are walking past you and whispering your name.

Or are they?

I just wanted to leave.

I wasn't tripping out my box or anything, but I just wanted to leave. Lynn wanted to stay, so I had to wait another hour or two until we were due to get the bus back. And I was dreading that bus.

I was dreading it because I didn't want people staring at me. Some of the buses were comfy coaches where all the seats faced forwards. But I could see that some of the buses were like normal double-deckers. And some of those double-deckers have got seats down the front that face backwards, they face the rest of the passengers. What if we got on that bus and all the seats were taken except for the ones that faced everybody? I'd have to sit there, facing everycunt, while I was tripping. And the lights inside those buses are on bright as fuck, there would be nowhere to hide. I'd be facing everybody, under bright as fuck light, and they'd be looking at that Limmy cunt. They'd be taking wee pictures or videos of that Limmy cunt looking out his box, looking pure para as fuck. They might even speak to me. Fucking hell, man. Cunts would be steaming, and they'd be looking for a giggle to pass the time. They'd speak to me, one after the other, and they'd film it. For an hour. Because that's how long that bus journey was back to Glasgow. An hour. Imagine an hour of that.

Fucking dreading it.

When Lynn was ready to go, we went to the bus queue. And thank fuck, it was a coach. A comfy coach. We got on, sat down, side by side, me at the window, not the aisle, not the aisle where people could see me. Then the driver shut the door, switched off the lights, and away we went. The lights going off, what a fucking relief.

When we got off at Buchanan Bus Station, we waited in the queue for the taxi. Folk walked by, and I thought I heard somebody say 'Requiem', a line from one of my videos. I turned around, but none of them looked at me. I didn't know if I was imagining it or not.

Then I bumped into some folk I knew from when I was a teenager.

Fuck right off.

I smiled and said I had a good time, thanks, aye. Then me and Lynn got in the taxi.

When I got home, I went into the kitchen for a drink of water. The lights were off, but there was a blue light coming from my computer, from the case, from an LED. I looked at my computer, and I felt an evil presence from it.

It didn't even bother me.

I'd taken so much acid in my younger years that it was nothing new. I had my chewing gum eccie experience as well, and the evil voice that wanted to harm that lassie and I had to fight against, and I had that experience with the poster of the sunflowers.

This thing with the computer was fuck all. It was just annoying. Like a fly.

I walked out the kitchen and thought, right, that's that.

That's the end of that.

Sunday 12th July 2009. The last time I took drugs. Get it all to fuck.

How to Make a Sketch Show

It was time to make the first series of *Limmy's Show*.

I've talked like fuck to you about all my feelings and all the suicidal stuff, but let's take a break from that and dive into something technical. Before making *Limmy's Show* it was a mystery to me how a person would go about writing and directing a sketch show, and maybe you're the same. Well, here it is. Don't worry, I'll come back to the suicidal stuff later.

Right, let me take that sketch about Dee Dee going to Yoker as an example again. It's from the second series, not the first, but because I've already told you how I got the idea I think it would be a good example to show you how it went from an idea to being a sketch on the telly.

The first thing I did was I listened back to the podcast episode, and typed a transcript as I went along, leaving out bits that didn't feel important or didn't feel that they'd work visually. Then I started turning the transcript into a script. Obviously, for most sketches, I wouldn't be doing a transcript from a bit of audio. I'd maybe just start with a bullet list of things that are important, then type up a script with those things in mind.

To type the script, I used something called Final Draft, and formatted it in the way that the BBC wanted.

If you look at their site, you'll see examples. I just copied that.

I broke down each part of the script into scenes, e.g. outside the broken-down bus; inside the bus; off the bus at Yoker, etc. Then I thought about what exactly would happen in each scene – the action, the dialogue, the voiceover and maybe the change of music.

Everything in that sketch was led by Dee Dee's voiceover, so most of what he said had to be shown, e.g. if he talked about seeing a couple of buses, I'd type in the action to describe it, like 'DEE DEE sees a couple of buses parked, with passengers coming off the front bus and going to the bus behind.' That would almost describe the shot, so I'd scribble down a wee storyboard picture for it, a simple stick-man thing. By the time I was finished I could read through the script and imagine all the shots and the timing of it all, and it all seemed to work. It came to about six minutes.

I didn't do storyboards for all the sketches, just a few of the complicated ones. For most of them I could just picture the shots by reading the script.

Then I sent all the scripts off to the Comedy Unit. They sent it to the commissioner, he said what he liked or didn't like, and fortunately he liked almost everything, including this Yoker sketch.

I then had a big meeting with all the crew to talk about the sketches.

This was the second series, so the look of Dee Dee was already established, but in the first series I spoke to the wardrobe and make-up people about how I saw Dee Dee, his hair and face and the clothes he wore; they came back and asked me if I meant this or that, and I'd say yes or no, or they'd come back with something different but it was better than what I had suggested.

The locations guy showed me pictures of where we could film, and he took me there. It turned out it was too tricky to film in Yoker, and that Clydebank had some better spots to park or drive. The Yoker bus terminus could be filmed outside Clydebank College, the bit where he goes to Hair by Les Porter could be filmed in Kelvindale, Dee Dee's flat could be filmed over in Summerston. All over the place.

Other people asked me things like how many passengers I needed for the buses, and what types of buses I meant exactly. The art department would ask me if I needed lots of signs for when Dee Dee said 'Yoker Post Office, Yoker F.C.,' etc. I said we could save time and effort if I just scrolled the names of the places past my face, in a more textual than realistic way. The sound guy wanted to know if I'd be speaking on the bus while it was moving. The first assistant director wanted to know if we could film in this place rather than that place because it would save time. Lots of questions. We then went for what's known as a tech recce, where you all go to the locations to see if there will be any technical problems with filming there. Then, not long after that, it was time to start filming.

Before filming the Yoker sketch, I wrote a shot list, which I learned in the first series by looking online and asking around amongst the crew. What you're aiming for with a sketch show, which has to be filmed quickly, is to have the least number of camera positions you can. Moving the camera around, moving lights, making sure everything looks fine in the background with that new angle – it all takes ages. To vary things, you can film different sizes of shot from that one camera position, e.g. film one take of Dee Dee as a wide shot (roughly head to toe), then film another take as a medium close-up (roughly head and shoulders).

I drew a floor plan of the broken-down bus scene at the start. I drew where Dee Dee would be, where the buses were, the passengers, all that. Then I scribbled down the camera positions I'd need to get all these shots. I wrote the number 1 in a circle for camera position 1, which would be facing Dee Dee as he walked past the buses, and below that I wrote a bullet list of 'WS Dee Dee until gets on bus, MS Dee Dee until gets on bus, CU Dee Dee thinking of getting on bus', with WS/MS/CU meaning wide shot, mid shot and close-up respectively. You won't need most of what you shoot, but you want to record more than you need, just in case.

Eventually I had a list of shots from each position, which I showed to the cameraman/director of photography and the first assistant director, so they knew how to light it or how long it would take to film.

By the time I turned up to film the thing, all the thinking and working out had been done. It was all there on paper, there was no guesswork. All the cast and the extras were there. I'd ask them to do this or do that, to look a certain way, to look more pissed off about the bus breaking down or whatever.

The first assistant director would shout 'Action!', rather than me, because I was acting in it, and we'd film that particular size of shot from that camera position. Then she'd shout 'Cut!' Then I'd have a look at the playback to see if it was what I was after. And if it was, we'd move on.

It took a day and a bit to film that entire sketch. On the first day it started getting late – and dark. If you watch the sketch and see the bit where the driver is waving the passengers onto the bus, you'll see that it's quite dark when they walk on. That was the end of the day. But when the bus is driving, it's all sunny and bright, because that was filmed earlier. I don't think anybody noticed, though.

We continued on to making other sketches. While we did that, the rushes (the footage) were sent off to the editor, who made a rough cut of how he saw the sketch being, based on my script. Because I hadn't turned up yet, he had to do the voiceover himself, which was funny to hear. I remember they had this English guy in once who did the temporary voiceover for my Falconhoof sketch where the guy shouts 'Jump the chasm!' This English guy pronounced chasm with an actual 'ch' sound, like the name Chas. I didn't mention it to him, though.

When I got to the edit, I did a new voiceover, and we started editing it more to my liking. I put in the music that I liked, these songs by The Orb that I used to listen to all the time when I was a tripper.

When all the sketches were finished, I looked at a big spreadsheet and made up a running order, where I'd decide which sketch went in which episode, and where in the episode it went. I put my favourite sketches in episodes early on in that particular series – or 'season', as you might call it – so that people would tune in to the following episode. I also had some of my favourites later on in the series, but I thought they'd be too dark or weird or non-funny to get people's attention. In an episode, I'd try to make sure there was a variety of sketch lengths and tones, by putting short sketches next to long sketches, quiet ones next to noisy ones, thoughtful ones next to daft ones, that kind of thing. The running order would then be sent off to the commissioner, who would maybe request for things to be shuffled a bit, because a favourite of his wasn't in the first episode, or the first episode contained one that wasn't a favourite. So I'd re-order things again. That could mean that one episode was now too short and one was too long (the episodes should be about 29 minutes long), and I'd have to maybe re-edit one of the sketches to make it shorter, or move sketches about from episode to episode. It could be quite a headache.

Once that was all agreed and locked down, we did the grade, which is when you fuck about with the contrast and the colours and all that. Then we went to the dub, the sound stuff, the final stage, where we'd do my absolutely final voiceover, plus put in any additional wee sounds and do the audio mixing. I say 'we', but I don't actually have my fingers on the mixing desk myself. It's these other cunts that do it, who know a lot more about stuff than I do.

Multiply that by however many other sketches and episodes were in *Limmy's Show*, and that's basically how a sketch show is made. How mine was made, anyway. It's a fucking buzz.

When you've prepared and prepared, and you know what you're doing, and people are all around you asking questions and you actually know what you're talking about for a change, and it's all go go go, and you're starting to see all these things you had in your head for months or years (or decades, when it came to the Yoker sketch), you're starting to see them all come to life ...

It's some buzz.

Mmm-hmm

It didn't all go smoothly, though.

I had a bit of a hiccup during the first series, during the prep stage.

By this point I'd written the series (it took me about six months), and I'd been allowed to direct it, for some mental reason. So there I was as this first-time director, excluding the pilot, meeting up with crew and trying to make a good impression. I wanted to make a good impression, not only in terms of making them feel like I knew what I was doing, but I wanted them to like me. I wanted us to all get on and have a good time, like one big happy family.

One of the props people came up to me, this guy just a bit older than me, and he wanted to ask me something about one of the sketches. It was a sketch called 'Mmm-hmm', where this guy is reading his newspaper but is interrupted by his wife, who wants to talk to him for a second. She then goes on this long rundown of how her day went, and he just responds by saying 'Mmm-hmm' throughout, like he's not listening. At the end, she notices, and says, 'You're not even listening. No you weren't. On you go, what was I saying then?' He proves he was listening by repeating everything she said, but in a far more concise manner. She lets him away with it, but he says, 'What, am I not getting an apology?', all pissed off. She says sorry. Then he lifts his newspaper up to block his face and get back to reading.

Kind of old-school 70s sexist comedy, when I think about it.

Anyway, this props guy was making the newspaper, because you can't just use a copy of the *Daily Record*. He wanted to know how I planned on filming the sketch, because it would determine whether he could get away with just designing and printing one side of the newspaper, or if he had to design and print both sides.

He showed me one that he'd already made. It was printed on the inside, but not the outside. I had a think about it. And unfortunately, the way I was going to film the sketch, the newspaper had to be printed on the outside, because it would be covering my face when I lifted it up.

I said to the props guy, 'No, it'll have to be printed on the outside, so that you see the front and back pages.'

He said 'Okay', and started writing a note.

I wasn't completely sure, though, and I didn't want to waste the guy's time. Remember, I was wanting to make a good impression. So I thought I'd double-check, just in case. I acted out that part of the sketch, the bit where I hold up the newspaper, to remind myself.

I said, 'What, do I not get an apology?' in this pissed-off voice.

The prop guy looked up from his notepad, all taken aback, and said, 'Sorry.'

He looked like I'd rolled up the newspaper and rapped it over his snout.

Oh dear.

I laughed and said, 'Fuck no, no, no. No, not you. It's the sketch, it's the last bit of the sketch, that's what the guy says.'

I expected the prop guy to burst out laughing as well, and say something like, 'Jesus, you had me worried there!' That's what you'd expect, wouldn't you?

But he didn't do that.

He didn't even smile.

He just looked back to his notepad, like I'd humiliated him. He asked another question or two, then he went away. He just couldn't laugh it off. It was like he couldn't yet recover from the shock of being spoken to like that, even after the misunderstanding had been explained. He just needed ten minutes to get over it.

But he never did.

That atmosphere was there between us for the whole five weeks of filming, I'm not fucking joking. He'd be having a laugh with the rest of the cast and crew, but then when he spoke to me, he'd switch.

I know you only get one chance to make a first impression, but fucking hell.

What It's Like Being on the Telly?

I've been asked a few times, 'What's it like being on the telly, with cunts coming up to you in the street? Cunts staring at you and that, what's it like?'

Well, I'll tell you.

The first series of *Limmy's Show* was on for six weeks, every Monday. I went up the toon one Saturday, during the run. I walked up Buchanan Street, one of the busiest shopping streets in Glasgow, at one of the busiest times of the busiest days.

Before I was on the telly, I'd maybe get recognised every month or two, providing I went to enough pubs and other places where the fans of my website would go. But walking up that street was something else.

It felt like everybody I passed was looking at me.

Anybody I looked at was looking at me.

The people nearby were looking at me. The people further away, over there, they were looking at me. And they were nudging the person next to them, so they'd look as well.

I made eye contact with a few, and smiled. I got some smiles back, but some didn't smile, they just looked, out of interest.

That was freaky.

That made me look down or look ahead to the distance. But I'd see heads turn out of the corner of my eye. I heard people say, 'There's Limmy,' or 'There's that guy from *Limmy's Show*,' or just '[Something something something] Limmy.'

Nobody was ripping my clothes off or anything, nobody was stopping me for a picture, but it got that intense that I had to just take a sharp turn and walk down a lane. I couldn't keep up the act that I didn't see or hear anybody, and I couldn't react to everybody by making eye contact and smiling or waving. I didn't know where to look or what to do, so I just fucked off down this lane and went a quieter way.

When the first series was finished, all that calmed down a bit. Then it would start up again when the next series was on. It calmed down after I finished all the telly stuff, after the third series, but then started up again with my Vines.

These days, people spot me and say hello or get a picture with me, which I like. I love folk coming up to me and I love chatting with them. There's been a few times when I've loved chatting with them so much that they have to make their excuses and walk away. You know, all that 'I'll let you go' patter.

Folk shout things from motors, catchphrases and that, or they just shout 'Limmy!' It's good seeing somebody smiling at you and saying hello because you made them laugh one night. It's kind of like those guys at the dealer's flat, but more often.

The more uncomfortable side of it is when people sometimes take sneaky pictures of me. I've been in cafés or wherever, and I see somebody pretend to be looking at their phone, but I can see they're lifting it too high. I can't wave at them, because they might actually just be looking at their phone, and I'd look mental. So I just have to sit there and pretend to not notice. It could just be nothing. But then other times I've been tweeted the picture later, by the person I saw take the picture, this person that didn't speak to me when I was right there in front of them.

It is kind of mental. But it also kind of helps if you're already mental. I mean, I've always been a bit para anyway, about people looking at me or thinking things about me. But if your paranoia is actually justified, if people really are secretly taking pictures of you like a mini kind of *Truman Show* or something, it sort of chills you out. You're less paranoid, and more 'Oh well.'

I've been on a train, with the guy sitting opposite watching me eating crisps. Not taking his eyes off me. I had to start a conversation with him to find out if he knew who I was or if he was just watching me eating crisps. Turns out he knew who I was, which is why he was watching me eating crisps.

I was on a flight to Spain a few months ago, and just as I've come out the toilet, there's this stag do shouting, 'There's Limmy!' Then this hen party looked and went, 'It is! No way! Are you Limmy?' I've just come out the toilet, and I'm para about them wondering if I've been in there for a pish or a shite or whatever. I said hello, and tried to make my way back to my seat, but the food trolley was in the way. I was standing there, waiting, all para, because I was wearing shorts, and I don't normally wear shorts, and I was wondering if they were wondering if I'd just done a shite.

I was in a hotel in Dundee, and somebody working at the reception recognised me, and I said hello. I went out for the night to do a show, and when I got back there were Maltesers on my bed, and a note from the staff saying they were big fans and here was a present. I thought that was thoughtful of them, but I also had my pants lying about the place. I wondered if they'd sniffed them, or took pictures of themselves wearing my pants on their heads.

So if you're wondering what it's like being on the telly, it's like that.

The IT Crowd

When the first series was on the telly, Graham Linehan had tweeted that he liked *Limmy's Show*, and me and him sent a few tweets back and forth. Not long after that, my agent got in touch and said that I'd been offered a part on *The IT Crowd*, if I was interested.

Which I was. I was a bit nervous about whatever the part would be, because I'd never really been on anybody else's thing before.

I looked up the programme, because I never watched it. I saw that there was the main cast, the three of them, but there were also these other bigshots that had small parts here and there. Chris Morris used to be in it, as their boss. And Noel Fielding sometimes made an appearance. I wondered if I'd be something like that, or something more. This could be my big break.

I got the script through, and read the part. It said I was to be a window cleaner. There were some words I was to say, but there were brackets above the dialogue that said something like, [This is a guide. Character speaks in unintelligible Glaswegian accent.]

My heart sank.

My big break on UK-wide telly was for me to go on and be a stereotypical Scot, like that C. U. Jimmy character by Russ Abbot. I mean, I think C.U. Jimmy is funny and everything, but … I don't know. Fuck.

I think my face went red with embarrassment, just thinking about it to myself. Don't get me wrong, I didn't find it offensive. But I had it in my head that I'd be asked to stretch myself a bit, because I'd done all these other characters for *Limmy's Show*. I imagined how it would go down with Scottish folk. I imagined me getting the piss taken out of me, by people calling me a sell-out.

I was pally with the guys from *Burnistoun* at the time, and I told them about it. I said I was going to do it, but I felt like a bit of an Uncle Tom. One of them said, 'An Uncle *Tam*,' and we pissed ourselves at that. An Uncle fucking Tam.

But I went down to London for the rehearsal in some hall. Graham was there, and all the cast. They were all friendly and smiley. Richard Ayoade was a bit quiet, though, but that's just the way he is. I remember there was a bit where we were watching this video of him that they recorded earlier, and I burst out laughing. I looked over at Richard while I was laughing, and he was just looking at me out of the corner of his eye, not smiling. I wondered if he was thinking, 'Who's this cunt?'

I got up and did my bit, acting it out with Chris O'Dowd. Graham liked it, but wanted a tweak here and there. I felt all vulnerable, having to do what somebody else wanted. I hadn't felt that on *Limmy's Show*, because I was so used to calling the shots myself. I sympathised with the actors from my series, because that's how it must have felt.

We filmed it on another day. I was a tiny bit nervous, but generally fine. But all the time I was thinking how this was going to go down in Scotland. Was I going to get slagged rotten for it?

That night I stayed at Matt Lucas's house. He'd also tweeted that he liked *Limmy's Show*, and he emailed to say that him and me and Graham could have dinner at his when I was down, and I could stay over. So I said aye. I never watched *Little Britain* that much, but I loved him as George Dawes on *Shooting Stars*.

That was mental when I first went to Matt's house, and he answered the door. There's me trying to act all normal, but all the time I'm thinking, 'It's fucking George Dawes from *Shooting Stars*.' It was a trippy feeling. It was the same with meeting the folk from *The IT Crowd*, shaking hands with these faces that I'd seen on the telly, but especially with Matt Lucas, because I was in his house.

Matt Lucas was very welcoming. No, we didn't shag, if that's what you're thinking, and it's out of order that you even thought that.

When the episode finally went out, I was bracing myself for a slagging. But people liked it. Nobody slagged me off, so I was happy. I'm glad I did it.

But the best thing about it was meeting these famous folk. That's one of the best things about having been on the telly, not just Graham Linehan and Matt Lucas, but these other folk I'd later come into contact with because of *Limmy's Show*. It's not because I'm now a part of their clique, nothing like that. I'm talking about that trippy feeling. I'm talking about even just being on a radio interview and there are some other recognisable people around the table, like her from that cooking programme, or her that presents stuff, or him that wrote that film that you sometimes see being interviewed.

It's that imposter syndrome thing, but in a good way. It's a feeling like I don't belong there, but I've sneaked in and nobody knows it. It reminds me of the feeling I used to have when I was wee and I'd sneak out the house at night and hide in gardens and watch people go by, that same wee thrill of them not knowing I was there. These famous people can see me, but they don't see the person inside, the one that's hidden away.

Trying for a Baby

I mentioned that Lynn wanted to have a baby.

When Lynn first told me she wanted to have a baby, it scared the life out of me. It was a horrible thing to hear.

She'd said it a few times. She'd hinted at it. We'd be watching a programme like *One Born Every Minute*, and she'd say something about how it's making her broody or something like that. I'd just keep my eyes on the telly and not say anything. I'd sense her head turning to face me, but I wouldn't look at her. I just wanted it to go away.

The idea honestly fucking terrified me.

I didn't want to have a baby. I wanted things to be just the way they were. Even the idea of getting a cat or a dog terrified me. That responsibility of looking after it constantly. But at least with a pet, if something happened to it, if it got hit by a bus or if it lost an eye or if it just died naturally, it would be a shame, but at least you'd get over it. How would you get over something like that if it happened to your own wean?

Fucking terrifying.

And what if something went wrong before it was even born? What about a miscarriage?

I was happy with my carefree life, where I was free to not care too much about anything, not care about myself, not care too much about Lynn because she can care about herself.

A baby?

No, no, no. No. A million and one things to worry about. A million and one things I don't know.

But eventually Lynn persuaded me, with a mixture of bad things and good. There were the usual arguments about how negative I was and how there wasn't much of a future for us if we both wanted different things. But then there were positive things, hopeful things, things about love and giving and warmth and all that. And that's what persuaded me the most. I said alright then. What a scary thing to say. What a scary thing to hear yourself say, to agree to have a wean. It was like when I agreed to do that first stand-up show. What a thing to agree to.

So we tried for a bit, and got nowhere.

Lynn thought it was something to do with my balls, because there was something wrong with them. I'd told her I was born with undescended testicles, and Lynn read that it can affect your sperm. Plus my balls are quite wee. They never hang down all that low to keep cool, and heat kills sperm.

I went for a sperm test at the doctor, and he phoned to say that it was bad. A low sperm count, and the sperm had deformed heads or something like that. He said that it looked like things like IVF wouldn't work either. It looked like the only way we could have a baby was if we got a sperm donor.

That was an upsetting thing to hear. A sperm donor. It was out of the question. It would feel like some other guy's wean, that's how I felt. That was my first thought. It would be some other guy's wean. I hoped to fuck that Lynn didn't persuade me to go through with it. And she could have if she wanted to. I was bracing myself for it. I was bracing myself for saying, 'Alright, if that's what you want,' and me going fucking numb as she walked about with a bump that didn't belong to me. Very negative thoughts. The worst of thoughts. Toxic masculinity, if that's what you want to call it. I tried to tell myself that it wouldn't matter, I'd get used to it. If I had met Lynn while she was pregnant with another guy, that would be fine somehow. Or if we adopted, that would be fine as well. But there was something about seeking out the sperm of another man, because mine wasn't good enough. There was something fucking heartbreaking about that. I tried to remember that the important thing was that we were bringing a wean up and making it happy and giving the wean love. That was the important thing. But another part of me was thinking about killing myself, if it came to it.

Lynn looked into something called ICSI. It's like IVF, but with IVF you just mix the sperm and egg together, whereas with ICSI you inject the sperm right into the egg. Which is perfect for lazy, shite sperm like mine.

We went to some private place and paid a few grand for them to do all that. Lynn had to inject herself with this stuff to overproduce eggs, which was tough on her body. All I had to do was go into a wee room in this place, and have a wank into a container. They had a wee folder of top-shelf magazines, and I had a wank over them. Then I walked out with my container, and a red face from wanking. What a funny way to bring a life into the world.

Lynn got pregnant, and I was delighted. I was also angry about that doctor. That fucking doctor, saying that IVF and all the rest of it wouldn't work either. How fucking irresponsible.

I was happy, though. But also scared. Now that we had this precious thing, we also had something to lose. I know, very negative, but the feeling of something going wrong made my skin crawl. Lynn was cool as a cucumber, not worried at all. But I was thinking what if?, what if?, what if?

What if there's something wrong with it? What if there's something wrong with my son or daughter and I can't fucking cope? What if it becomes so stressful and so sad that I can't cope? What then? There are other people who cope, and I don't know how they fucking do it, because I couldn't. I'm just not fucking strong enough. What will happen?

We went for a 4D scan, and everything was fine. We didn't ask what sex it was, but we thought it looked like a boy. I was pretty sure. I looked at his face moving. His brow was like mine, sort of sloping down at the outside. I was saying to Lynn and the nurse that the scan was amazing. But I couldn't shake off that worry. My son here that I was looking at, was he going to be alright? What if there was something wrong with his brain? What if he had some condition that … I don't know. Something.

I'd lie in bed thinking about how our son was going to turn out, if he'd be alright. And I thought something that made me feel better, something that probably most normal people think all by themselves, it probably comes to them naturally. I thought to myself, look, it's not about you. It's about him. It's about your son. He needs you. You're here for him, he's not here for you. You're here for him, and he'll need you. And that's all you need to do. If anything goes wrong and your life doesn't turn out the way you didn't think it would, well, it's not about you now. It's about him. It's not about what's happening to you, it's about what's happening to him. You'll have no room to worry about yourself and how you feel, if you devote yourself to how he feels.

That made me feel better.

I'd never felt so selfless before. I know how daft that sounds. It sounds vain, like I'm talking about all my charity work, and it probably doesn't sound that selfless at all to you. But for me it was. I mean selfless in an almost spiritual sense. It was like I wasn't here, not here for me anyway. I'm here for something else. The feeling took me out of myself.

Lynn went into labour.

It was the wee hours of the morning. I jumped out of bed and phoned a number I was given. We'd been going to these antenatal classes at the hospital, and I was worried about the fact that I didn't drive, and I'd asked if we should just get a taxi or if there was some other NHS service. The woman at the class told me that a taxi probably wouldn't take us in case Lynn made a mess, so she gave us the number for this type of maternity ambulance that would pick us up. I had that number on me all the time; I was very well prepared. I phoned it, and they said that they wouldn't pick us up, that's not what they did. I said that we were told to phone this number, but the person on the phone said no, that's not what they did. So I had to phone a taxi, expecting the driver to turn up and see Lynn going into labour and drive away without us. But he took us. The fucking opposite of what that woman at the class told us. Thanks for that. Thanks, and thanks to that doctor who said I'd never get Lynn pregnant. Thank you both.

We got there, and everything went just how you'd expect, like *One Born Every Minute*. All the time I was thinking, 'Don't die. Don't let my son come out dead.'

I tried helping by saying 'breathe' to Lynn, but she said, 'Stop saying that.' I had a feeling she would, but I wanted it down on record that I at least tried to help.

Eventually, my son's head came out of Lynn (with his head still attached to the rest of his body). The midwife asked me if I wanted a look, so I looked. And there was a baby's head sticking out of Lynn's fanny. It was a strangely normal sight.

He came out, I cut the cord, and he lay against Lynn's chest, looking into Lynn's eyes. Then she was taken away to get stitched up, while I watched him in his wee cot, all wrapped up.

I felt quite calm. I wasn't in tears of joy, I didn't whisper to him, 'I will look over you, little one,' nothing like you'd see in a film. It just all felt strangely normal, with an undercurrent of worry.

Daniel McGowan Limond, born 30th August 2010. Welcome to life.

Please don't turn out like me.

Twitter Trouble: Punch

When I say that I hope my son doesn't turn out like me, I mainly mean that I hope he doesn't turn out to be a worrier. I worried like fuck throughout that pregnancy.

A few days before Lynn gave birth, we were sitting in the living room watching the telly. I was a bit bored for a few seconds, so I tweeted something out of order, to perk me up. I tweeted something like, 'I just hooked the jaw of my pregnant girlfriend.'

I know, I know.

Why do I joke about things like that? I don't fucking know. Maybe because it was the opposite of how I wanted things to be. Right here and now, that joke turns my stomach a bit, because I'm not in the same frame of mind. When I read it now, in this frame of mind, it reminds me of news articles that I've read of guys who really have done things like that. I can't see any humour in it whatsoever. Even as a joke, I come across as somebody who would find news articles like that funny.

At the time of me tweeting it, it felt funny because it was the opposite of how things were. Things were nice and cosy and happy and me and Lynn were having a laugh and being cheeky and watching the telly. And then I fancied tweeting something like that.

I tweeted it, to what I think was about 10,000 followers. Nobody said anything. They were used to me coming out with horrible things. Fantasy things. Horror stories. Bad things that popped into my mind.

One lassie tweeted Lynn, saying something like, 'Is that true? #hopeyoureokay.' Me and Lynn had a laugh about that, because imagine this lassie actually thought I'd done that, and she's expressing concern with a hashtag.

Anyway, that was that.

The next day, I was away to some video editing place for something, and Lynn phoned me. She told me that she just had a reporter from the *Sun* at the door, asking about that tweet.

I was like, 'You fucking joking?'

A reporter had come to the door and asked if I really did hit her, and if she was alright. Lynn said that of course she was alright, it was just a joke.

The reporter said, 'Sorry, I don't get the joke, and that's funny how?' Almost criticising Lynn.

Lynn said, 'I don't know, you have to ask him.' And she shut the door on the guy. Then she phoned me.

I laughed and said, 'Jesus Christ.'

But Lynn said, 'It's not fucking funny, Brian. I'm about to give birth and I've got some fucking guy from the *Sun* at the door.'

I said sorry, and thought about how stress could maybe harm our son. I felt guilty, but also pissed off. I was a wee bit pissed off with myself for being naïve, but more pissed off with this *Sun* guy, because I knew he didn't give a fuck about Lynn, really, he just wanted an article.

The guy ended up phoning me about ten minutes later.

He introduced himself, and asked me to explain the tweet. I explained that my followers know I talk a lot of shite, and I like to come out with out-of-order things to entertain myself, I don't know why.

He asked me if I thought that domestic violence was funny. I felt like giving a sarcastic reply and saying, 'I think domestic violence is fantastic,' but then I reckoned he would quote me out of context. So I said, 'No.' Then I asked him not to come around to my flat again, because his visit caused my girlfriend some stress. I know, I had a cheek considering I caused it all, but still.

The next day there was an article in the *Sun* saying that I had been SLAMMED for my 'joke'. The reporter brought my tweet to the attention of a domestic violence charity and asked them to comment, and they criticised me. Lynn told me that her dad would see that article, and I felt like such a fucking arsehole.

After Lynn gave birth, we still hadn't thought of a name for our son, so I made a wee joke about naming him after my favourite character in *Street Fighter IV*,

Sagat, because I'd been playing the game all the time. I said on Twitter and on Facebook that I'd be calling him Sagat, or Tiger Uppercut McGowan Limond (because Sagat shouts 'Tiger uppercut!').

It was fuck all to do with that joke about me punching Lynn. But the day after Lynn gave birth, the *Sun* did another article saying I was now a dad, and I was going to call my son 'UPPERCUT' (caps and bold), days after me 'sparking fury' with my punching joke.

I thought, 'Oh, you fucking cunts.'

When I went into hospital, I saw that copy of the *Sun* in the reception, and I saw the article. I wondered how many other people in the hospital had seen it and thought I was a bad person. I was pissed off with the *Sun* and pissed off with myself.

So I just opened up Twitter and I went like that, delete. I deleted the whole account, before I said something else stupid, something about the reporter, something that would get me the jail.

Limmy's Show, UK-wide!

After I was told that I'd be getting a second series of *Limmy's Show*, I was told that somebody at the BBC down south wanted to meet me, a commissioner. The chat would be about the possibility of my second series being on the network. That is, UK-wide, not just in Scotland. That would be fucking excellent. UK-wide telly, like all the bigshots.

I went down to London and met this commissioner at Television Centre, that old, famous BBC building, the one with the round bit in the middle. It felt good being in it, having seen it on the telly for decades. A landmark.

The commissioner told me that she liked my series and what she liked about it, and I said thanks. And she asked me about my background, how it all came about, how I got into it, that kind of thing. I was happy to go on about myself, but I was conscious of whether or not I was saying the right thing to get my second series on the network. I was wondering if I'd be given the decision during that meeting. I was just wanting to find out one way or another, I was just wanting her to get to the bit where I got told the news. It was like the *Antiques Roadshow*.

We talked a bit more, then she asked me a question. I reckoned that how I answered this question would decide if I was going UK-wide or not.

She said something along the lines of this: 'Now, I have to ask you, and please forgive me if this is offensive in any way. I showed your series to some of the people on the floor here to see what they thought, and for some of them, due to your dialect and your accent – and again, forgive me if this is offensive – but due to that, some of the words and punchlines went over their head. Just some wordings they weren't familiar with. Afterwards, they were able to work out what had been said, but timing is important in comedy, as you know, so they missed the joke at the crucial time. I suppose I'm saying this because I'm wondering how you feel about that.'

I thought about how to answer it, because I didn't want to fuck things up. But I said to her: 'Well, I get what you're saying. I don't find it offensive. If they can't understand some of my words, then they can't understand them, they're unfamiliar with them, I get that. But the reason they're unfamiliar with them is because, well, they don't hear people like me on the telly. They only hear people like themselves, or they might hear somebody from a region in northern England. I'm familiar with all those accents, and familiar with certain words and phrases, like "Come 'ed" in *Brookside*, or even "Fair dinkum" in *Neighbours*. *Neighbours* is Australian. It can't be right that I know words and phrases from the other side of the world, but words and phrases from another UK nation are an issue. I know the Glaswegian dialect is a bit harder to crack, but I think the solution is to have more accents and dialects on the telly, rather than fewer.'

I knew I was risking things by coming out with that, but I had to stand my ground. It's supposed to be the British Broadcasting Corporation, representing all of

Britain. Why should I be the one to change who I am? And if I didn't get my second series on the network, so be it. I could live with that.

Except that's not what I said.

It's what I wish I'd said.

When she asked how I felt about my accent, what I really said was, 'I see, I see. Well, I mean, there are ways to maybe, I don't know, tone down the dialect a bit. Ways to tone it down without it looking like I'm speaking all properly.'

I sold my soul.

Because when I got back home, I got told a while later that the second series wouldn't be going out UK-wide. I don't know why.

So not only did I sell my soul, but I sold it for fuck all.

Worth a shot.

Being a Dad

I wasn't coping with being a dad.

Despite not doing anything, despite it being Lynn that was up at all hours feeding him and looking after him, and her organising visits to the doctor and wee classes he could go to, and absolutely everything else – despite all that, I wasn't coping.

I had no fucking idea just how much having a baby would eat into my time.

I'd been so used to being lazy. I'd been so used to doing fuck all, to lying on the couch on a Sunday and watching *Columbo*, or jumping on the computer and doing a wee After Effects tutorial, or playing a game, or quite simply doing nothing. Doing fuck all had been very important to me. Not having to care about anybody had been a big part of me. And now all that had changed.

I couldn't be seen relaxing. If I was, Lynn would want me to do something, because she'd been up all night and she was knackered. I completely understood, but my mind was always on these other things I wanted to do. I just could not fucking switch off, I couldn't get the fidgetiness out of my head, I couldn't settle into it. I couldn't shake that selfishness.

It wasn't always hard. I liked relaxing with Daniel or feeding him. I liked looking at him and going up close. But other times it got very boring. Very, very boring. He didn't have a personality yet. He was just a baby that had to be kept alive.

When I thought I had a minute to myself, I'd sneak off to do some wee hobby, to do fuck all. But then I'd be asked what I was doing, and I'd have to stop. And I fucking hate having to stop something when I've just got into it. Fucking hate getting pulled away.

Trying to be an unselfish person was driving me insane. It felt like it was against my nature. It felt like something was wrong with me, like I wasn't wired for it. It was like smoke was coming out my ears. I don't know if you've ever had a vacuum cleaner that has something wrong with it, the suction isn't working that well, but it's making a fucking racket, then you start to smell some kind of smoke, and you touch the thing and it's roasting, then it conks out. That's what my brain was like.

I'd do some stuff, though. I'd take him out in his pram, and go for a walk. We'd go into a restaurant for lunch, just me and him. I'd wait outside till he was asleep so he didn't start crying, then I'd go in. Right after ordering for myself, he'd wake up and need his nappy changed, and I'd have a meltdown taking him to the toilet with the wet wipes and doing all that and bringing him back to his pram and me trying to eat my food while he was crying, then I'd just go, 'Fuck it,' and leave, with my food hardly touched.

We'd go for a walk about, and I'd be para about things falling on him from tenement flats above, like fags or bird shite. I didn't want him burned or blinded. I'd be para about exhaust fumes. I'd be para about fucking everything.

I didn't know how single parents coped, I didn't know how they fucking did it. My head was melting, and I was barely contributing a thing. Lynn was practically a single parent. I contributed fuck all.

Well, no, I did do one thing.

Daniel didn't like falling asleep. He'd cry to try and fight it, and we'd have to spend ages shooshing him – ages. It was driving Lynn mental. But then I came up with a revolutionary technique. I was lying in bed with him, with me lying on my back with my legs bent, a bit like if you were to do sit-ups, and he was lying back against my legs with his head at my knees. And I started bobbing my hips up and down. It was like bobbing a wean in your arms, except you're doing it with your crotch (it's not something I'd do in public). It meant I had my arms free, to hold Daniel's hands, or look at my phone. When he started to nod off, I'd stop bobbing. If he was in my arms, I'd have to stand there for ages until I was sure he was asleep, but by lying on my back I got to relax. I could even nod off myself, which was perhaps dangerous, but all that ever happened was he'd nearly fall on a comfy bed a few inches below.

Lynn tried it, and she said it was a lifesaver. It was a miracle.

I reminded her of that contribution of mine every few days. It was like that time my company got that Creative Futures award, because of Limmy.com. I'd bring it up any time I felt like a useless dad, just every now and then.

I still bring it up.

Limmy's Show, Series 2

I'd been given a second series, and I was wanting to make things different. The reception to the first series of *Limmy's Show* had been mixed – I'd been looking online to see what people thought. There were people who thought the entire series was shite, and I could dismiss those comments; the comments I was interested in were the ones that went something like 'I liked *Limmy's Show*, but ...'

The 'but ...' stuff tended to be comments about some sketches being too slow and drawn out or too quiet. I'd read that stuff and nod, because I agreed. I knew the sketches were like that, though. I didn't want them to be all fast and noisy, I wanted something weird rather than something that assaulted the senses. I'm sure there were some people who liked all the weirdness, but I was seeing too many of these comments about it being slow and quiet.

I started watching an American sketch show called *Tim and Eric Awesome Show, Great Job!*, which had been recommended to me a few times, but I'd never got round to watching it. I thought it was hilarious. It was cheap looking, cheaper looking than mine, but it was packed with stuff, it was fast as fuck, the editing was fast, it was noisy, there was music everywhere, stupid sound effects, it was hilarious and weird and clever.

I thought, right, *Limmy's Show* is going to be more like that.

Some stuff won't change, things like Dee Dee and Falconhoof will have the same pace and style, but the other stuff is going to change, it's going to be dafter, there's going to be music everywhere, sketches are going to be shorter and split into pieces, some of them will merge with other seemingly unrelated sketches, it'll be edited quicker, shots will be shorter, they'll be short as fuck, and it'll be up to viewers to keep up, I will have no cunt saying that's too slow, no cunt will say that it's too quiet or too slow or that it loses energy or anything like that, it'll be bang bang bang, and it'll be me saying to them, 'What's the matter, pal, can you not keep up? Are you too *slow*?'

I would change the way I wrote it, the way I directed it, and I made the radical decision to change the cast. I wanted a complete change of everything. I wanted a brand new feeling to it. The cast were told that it was nothing personal or anything like that, because if there was ever a third series, then I'd swap the cast again, no matter what. I hoped that would make them feel better knowing that, if they felt bad about my decision. I auditioned a new cast. I was scared that I wouldn't be able to find anybody, but I loved the new cast, thank fuck.

When it came to making the second series, I felt like a better director than in the first. My decisions were quicker, I took more shortcuts, I knew more about what I needed to film and what I wouldn't, everything felt easier and more fun, it just felt like more of a laugh.

In the edit, I was saying to the editor, 'Could you trim that bit? Even more than that. No, even more than that.' All the time I was thinking of folk who said the first series was too slow. I was saying, 'Trim that bit so it just goes straight into that next bit. Honestly, I don't want to give these cunts a chance to breathe.'

I didn't want to give you cunts a chance to breathe.

When it was finally aired, I felt that the reception was much better than before. Nobody was saying it was slow. It had tons more energy, it was just what I was wanting. But one thing that was important to me was how it compared to *Burnistoun*. After our first series aired, people were saying they preferred *Burnistoun* to *Limmy's Show*, it was a more upbeat sketch show, it was livelier, it was funnier – and it had about twice the viewing figures. Although I didn't want to make a mainstream sketch show like that, the more people saying they preferred my sketch show to theirs the better, because I'm a competitive cunt like that.

Well, when my second series came out I noticed more people saying just that. People who preferred their first series to mine, now preferred my second series to theirs, and I was happy to hear it. And when the Scottish BAFTAs came in 2011, and I was up against *Burnistoun* and I won, I was happy. Well, I wasn't happy that I won, it didn't mean that much to me by itself, but I was happy that I didn't lose, and didn't lose to them.

I was so happy with how the second series went that when I was told that I was getting a third series I didn't want to change a thing. I didn't want to change the cast, like I said I would. So I didn't. When the third series aired, with the same cast as before, I imagined how the cast from the first series felt about that, after maybe having told people, 'He let us go because he'd be changing the cast every series, it was nothing personal,' and then they see the third series with the same cast from the second. I felt like a right lying prick.

But I was so happy with that second series. And if you want to know my favourite episode, I'd maybe say the second one, because it's got the Yoker sketch, the Tina Turner dancing competition one, and the sketches about Marti Pellow. They're all sketches that felt ambitious for me to film because they were long or technically difficult or different from my other sketches, and all of them went down well.

Things felt very good at that time.

Meeting Charlie Brooker

Some more bigshots tweeted that they liked *Limmy's Show*, one of them being Charlie Brooker. I was like that to Lynn, 'Look who's tweeted about *Limmy's Show*. Charlie Brooker!'

I was very excited. I liked Charlie Brooker's stuff, and I liked him as well. Plus he had tons of followers.

I was even more excited when my agent got in touch and said that Charlie Brooker wanted to work with me. He wanted me to do something for *Screenwipe*, plus there was some new thing he was making and he was wondering if I wanted to contribute to that as well.

Fucking amazing.

A meeting was arranged down in London, and down I went to meet him.

We met in this private club place during the daytime. It wasn't like that shitey private club in Edinburgh, back when I met that Dracula cunt. This one was like an upmarket bar or restaurant, and it was busy. Me and my agent went over to a booth where Charlie was sitting with somebody from his company. I was all pleased to meet him.

He said that he liked my stuff, and I said that I liked his. I liked *Screenwipe*, and I liked *Nathan Barley*. When I mentioned *Nathan Barley*, I remembered to ask him a question that had been on my mind ever since I saw it.

I wondered if he'd based a particular bit on something from my Limmy.com.

D'you remember I said that one of the first play-things on Limmy.com was this shagging machine called Come Again? Well, in it, whenever you did the shagging, it would make these female shagging sounds, like 'Uhhh! Uhhh!' And for the background music, I had '(Keep Feeling) Fascination' by The Human League. Well, there was this bit in *Nathan Barley* where he's playing with something on his phone, making these shagging sounds. And then there's this other bit where he speaks to the camera, quoting a bit of the chorus to 'Fascination'. I thought that was some coincidence, that. Plus the fact that the Nathan Barley character himself is this idiot with a website, trying to promote it everywhere and make a name for himself, which folk like me used to do.

When I saw the episode, I wondered if he happened to stumble upon Limmy.com when he was writing *Nathan Barley*, looking for examples of wanks with websites, and he scribbled down a few notes after seeing Come Again. There had been no way to ask him before. But now, here he was, right in front of me.

So I asked him. 'Here, I've been meaning to ask.' And I described the whole thing to him. And I said, 'Did you get that from my site at all?'

And he said no. He wasn't familiar with my site.

Oh well.

Anyway, he told me that he'd like me to contribute something to his end-of-year *Screenwipe*, which I ended up doing.

But it was this other thing he was working on that sounded very interesting. He said he was going to be making an anthology series, a series where each episode is a different story, kind of like *The Twilight Zone*. I said I loved *The Twilight Zone*, which he did as well. We were making wee *Twilight Zone* references during the conversation that only true experts in the *Twilight Zone* would get, and it was good to click with somebody I'd potentially be working with, especially concerning this anthology thing.

He told me about one of the episodes he'd written. It was about how somebody had kidnapped a member of the royal family, and the only way they'd be released without harm is if the prime minister shagged a pig, live on the telly.

As you've probably guessed, this anthology series he was going to make was *Black Mirror*. Everybody knows it as this dark vision of a possible future, with an element of humour in certain episodes. But the way I interpreted this idea he was telling me, I thought it was going to be more of a farce, a bit stupid, kind of laughable. So when he asked me if I wanted to write an episode, I thought along those lines.

A few weeks later I emailed him my idea. I didn't type up a script or big outline. It was just a rough idea.

And here was my idea. I can't remember how I worded it, but it was something like this.

It's set in the future.

And everything's gone wrong.

Crime is at an all-time high, so they had to do something about it. So they brought in this new rule, this new law. And it was this simple …

All crime is punishable by death. It's that kind of scenario. All crime is punishable by death or life imprisonment. Even dropping litter.

But!

There's this knife. This Rambo knife.

And anybody who has this knife is allowed to do anything they want with it.

You could stab the Queen, if you wanted, and you wouldn't spend a single day behind bars. People could try and stop you, maybe, but if you managed to do it, or did anything with this knife, you wouldn't get done for it.

The knife was kind of like a safety valve for society.

Anyway, the knife has been in the possession of these gangster types for years and years, so they can murder folk and get away with it.

But then it accidentally falls into the hands of an idiot. It falls off the back of a lorry, or out the window of the head gangster's armoured vehicle, and it lands in the hands of this idiot. A buffoon. I mean like a fucking

George Formby or Norman Wisdom type of guy, the type that trips over his own feet.

And … that's it. It's about what happens next.

I emailed him the idea, to see what he thought.

He replied saying that it wasn't up his street. It didn't really match with the theme of the rest of the series.

That was my big chance of writing for *Black Mirror*, a series that has now become iconic, a series that is as big now as *The Twilight Zone* was back in the day. People these days refer to things as being like something from *Black Mirror*, the way they used to do about *The Twilight Zone*. That was my big chance of being a part of that history.

And I give him George Formby with a Rambo knife.

But he did say that if I had any other ideas, I should send them over. I said that was no bother, and I'd have a think. I had a think, but I couldn't come up with anything else. That was the best idea I had.

I'm sure he'd still be up for having a look at any other ideas I've got, but I'm having trouble topping that one.

I should maybe send him it again, except now that I know what *Black Mirror*'s all about, I could tweak it to be more *Black Mirror*y. The exact same idea, a George Formby buffoon type, immune from prosecution, going about with a Rambo knife …

But it's a *virtual* Rambo knife!

Twitter Trouble: Die Now, Thatcher

In November 2011, as I was writing the third series of *Limmy's Show* (I think), I tweeted some things that nearly fucked up my career. Remember that I deleted my Twitter account to stay out of trouble? Well, I started up a new one, and got into trouble again.

It was in the news that FIFA had banned England players from wearing the poppy, and Prince William had got involved, asking for them to reconsider. So I tweeted, 'Would Prince William write to FIFA on behalf of the Scotland team wearing poppies? No. Cos he thinks ENGLAND won the war.'

I partly meant it, and partly just felt like saying something for a reaction.

I went a step further and tweeted, 'I'd love to slide a samurai sword up Prince William's arse to the hilt, then yank it towards me like a door that won't fucking open.'

Well, I got a reaction. All these Tories started having a go. Now that I had their attention, I changed my profile picture to this picture I made of Thatcher. She was still alive then, so I got a picture of her and wrote over it 'DIE NOW' in red. And I used the red pen to cut across her throat and scratch out her eyes and put all these slashes over her face. I wanted to make these Tory cunts feel outraged. I don't like Thatcher. To put it simply, I think she was a very cold-hearted person that did things that led to a lot of misery, and I don't like how these Tories admired her. I wanted to hurt them in some way.

Louise Mensch stepped in, who was this big Tory MP at the time. She wrote an article for the *Telegraph*, calling for the BBC to have nothing more to do with me. How could you justify giving licence fee money to this horrible person who wants an elderly lady to die?

I shat it. She had a point. Then again, this was Thatcher I was talking about. That might not matter, though. I might get told by the BBC to fuck off. This might be it. And then what? What would I do next? Go back to stand-up? Back to making websites?

I got an email from somebody advising me to apologise, so I did. I said sorry. Sorry for causing offence, it was never my intention to offend. When I did that, some people on Twitter told me I should never apologise for a joke, and that they were disappointed in me. But at the end of the day, those people don't pay my mortgage.

And to be fair, if you're forced to pay the licence fee, you're going to want the money going to decent people. You're maybe going to want to hold them to high standards of behaviour.

But the funny thing is …

Jeremy Clarkson punched his producer at the BBC. He put the guy in hospital. Clarkson allegedly called the producer a 'lazy, Irish cunt', and Clarkson was taken to court for a racial discrimination and personal injury claim, for which he had to pay £100,000 to the producer.

And yet …

Louise Mensch defended him. Defended Jeremy Clarkson, I mean.

And it just so happens that Jeremy is a Tory, like Louise.

Funny, that, isn't it?

Same sort of thing happened years later when I joked about Trump getting assassinated. Do you remember that?

On the 19th of January 2017, the day before Trump's inauguration, I tweeted, 'Looking forward to Trump's assassi … inauguration'

It was retweeted by this far-right guy who had about half a million followers at the time, where he criticised me. I then got tweeted by tons of his American followers, calling for me to be arrested. They copied in the FBI, the Secret Service, all that. They weren't joking. These were people with Trump all over their profiles, 'Proud patriot', all that shite.

They said it was a death threat, and I should get banged up for it. I was a bit worried, because a guy once got arrested for joking about bombing an airport. It could be me next.

I ended up in the papers for it, but nobody really cared. One or two people mentioned it when I was out and about, but it was to say to me that they thought it was funny as fuck.

And it was funny, how it turned out.

But here's the funny thing.

See that far-right guy that criticised me, see these people who wanted me arrested, see if you look at their bios on Twitter, it says they're 'Pro free speech'.

Haha!

My First Sitcom

As I was about to start writing the third series of *Limmy's Show*, I got the feeling that I didn't want to do *Limmy's Show* any more, and I wanted to get into writing a sitcom. I just wasn't feeling the ideas coming to me as quickly, not as quickly as they did for the second series. I wasn't coming up with any new big characters, like how I came up with Raymond Day and Larry Forsyth for the second series. And I was struggling a bit to come up with something for Dee Dee, Falconhoof and Jacqueline. I eventually did come up with stuff that I liked, but I had the feeling that if I ever did a fourth series I'd be writing a lot of shite. So it was time to move on to something new.

I worked with this production company down south on this idea that I had. The idea was that there was this pub, a shithole pub that opens up at 8 a.m., and this alky goes in for a drink. Not long after he sits at the bar, these various characters come in, separately, these folk from different walks of life that this alky regular guy has never seen before. They sit at the bar, each of them looking borderline suicidal. So the old alky asks them what their stories are. They tell him, and he tells them his story, and it's all told in flashbacks. It's kind of like a sitcom version of the old horror anthologies you used to get.

I fucking hated writing it. I hated trying to tie this whole story together, rather than just write sketches. I liked the challenge in a way, the feeling that I might make something good, but I hated feeling like I was maybe not very good at writing sitcoms, all that character arc shite. I took an interest in all these articles online about story beats and the inciting incidents and three acts or five acts and reversals and all that. I watched sitcom episodes and broke them down into the plot points, the bare essentials, and noted how many minutes into the episode they appeared – *Only Fools and Horses*, *Curb Your Enthusiasm*, *Seinfeld*, etc. I did all this analytical stuff. And it did my fucking nut in.

Then there was the back and forth with the production company, the notes. They all made sense, but I started not knowing if the sitcom was any good or not. I didn't know if the sitcom was something that I myself would watch. What a feeling that is, when you don't know if you like your thing any more. I never had that with *Limmy's Show*. I loved the lot of that.

But I grafted away to try and make it work, until I was happy. And we sent it off to the BBC.

I was expecting a knock-back, but I got asked to go down to the BBC in London for a meeting about it.

I said to Lynn that it would probably be a knock-back, I just knew it. But she said I was being negative. They wouldn't get me all the way down just to say no. They knew I was in Glasgow. The train took four and a half hours down, and four and a half hours back. Nine hours on a train. They'd just email or tell my agent or something.

So I went down, not trying to get my hopes up. Me and a couple of folk from the production company went into the BBC, that same building from when I was about to sell my soul to get my second series of *Limmy's Show* on the network. And it was the same commissioner.

She said that she really liked the sitcom. She liked how it was different from a lot of the other stuff going around. It was almost poetic, she said, the way things were worded.

But ...

She saw it more as a comedy drama. And that's not what they were looking for at the moment. She said I wasn't to change a thing, it was perfect the way it was, but it just wasn't what they were looking for at that time.

So it was a no.

Nine hours on a train, for that.

Nine hours, not including the underground and the waiting about, for a knockback that took ten minutes max. She could have just phoned. It would have taken ten seconds. But maybe she wasn't familiar with the telephone. It is Scottish, after all.

Anyway, I said I was sorry to hear that, but thanks for considering it. We said goodbye and I got up to leave.

Then she asks the production company guy, 'Oh, while you're here, would you mind staying behind for a quick chat?', and she said she wanted to chat about another production they were working on, one that was nothing to do with me.

I said to the production company guy, 'Will I just wait outside then?' And he said yeah, if I didn't mind.

I stood outside the room, while they chatted about this other production.

He eventually came out, we said, 'Oh well,' and I went back up to Glasgow, on my four-and-a-half-hour train.

Four and a half hours down, four and a half hours back. Nine hours all in. In fact, if you throw in the time on the underground and the waiting about, you may as well call it ten.

Hell

Here, am I starting to sound a bit grumpy? Do I sound like I'm in a bad mood?

Maybe I'm picking it up from how I felt at that time. A bit of a bad patch. I was 37, it was late 2011, early 2012, and things were getting on top of me.

I was writing the third series of *Limmy's Show*, and writing a sitcom pilot at roughly the same time. I was having trouble with both of them, and I'd walk about in a trance trying to think of things, just like I did back when I wrote that Glasgow Comedy Festival show in 2008.

I wouldn't be there for Lynn or Daniel, I'd always be thinking of something else, thinking about how I was going to make it all work out. Me and Lynn would get into arguments because I was being a shite boyfriend and dad, shiter than usual. I'm usually self-centred and inconsiderate at the best of times. I rarely come up with ideas for things we could do or put their interests before mine, unless I'm reminded; it's almost like I forget to care. But when I get in that bad way, walking about in a trance and worrying, my selfishness is less forgetful and more deliberate. I pull up the drawbridge. And you just can't do that when you're a boyfriend and a dad. It makes things worse. Me and Lynn would argue, and that would then make it harder for me to write, because

I wouldn't be in a good frame of mind, and that would make me worry even more, making me a shiter boyfriend and dad. It just went round and round like that, like before.

After one particular argument one night, I went into the toilet, and I thought about topping myself. I was either crying or close to crying, and I thought about just cycling down to the Clyde and jumping in. Just drowning in the freezing-cold water.

I thought, 'No, don't. Go for a cycle, though. Get out, go for a cycle, get a change of scenery.' But then I pictured myself cycling near the Clyde, and I saw myself not being able to stop myself from just getting off the bike and vaulting over that fence.

I kept thinking, 'Do it. Just do it. Kill yourself. Just get it over with. You can't do this any more, just do it. You keep coming back to this, sooner or later, you'll always come back to this. You're useless to her and useless to him, kill yourself before he's old enough to remember you. See if there are any teenagers down there at the Clydeside, get into a fight and goad them into throwing you in. Make it look like a murder. Or just go down and kill yourself. If you don't, you'll always come back to this.'

That's how it felt. It felt like I would always come back to that feeling. It was like a big, invisible elastic band. I could walk away and make the effort to feel good or content or at peace with things, but sooner or later I would be pulled back to this. It was like my default state. It was like I was meant to kill myself. Everything else was an effort. Suicidal feelings felt like coming home. They almost brought me closer to myself, they felt stronger than other feelings, they were intimate and private, they almost felt like when I used to spend all that time by myself when I was younger. But when I was suicidal I wasn't happy. I wasn't at peace. It didn't feel like a relief. I didn't want to do it, but I felt that I had to. I felt like I had no fucking choice.

I decided that I was going to do it.

I was going to go out for a cycle, go down to the Clyde and jump in. And I'd hopefully be so cold that I couldn't swim and I'd drown, and that would be the end of it. That would be the end of it.

I thought about it for a moment. I gave it a few moments. And I still felt that way. I was going to do it.

And the strangest thing stopped me.

I was so sure that I was going to do it, I was so sure that I was going to be dead in about half an hour, that I wondered what would happen afterwards. It wasn't the same as when I was going to top myself before, the day that I stopped drinking when I thought about what would happen afterwards to everybody I left behind. This time, I wondered what would happen to me. To my life. To my soul.

What's strange about that is that I'm an atheist. I don't believe in gods or an afterlife or spirits or souls or any of that. I'm not just the type of atheist that says, 'I don't believe in that, but who knows?' I was confident about my beliefs. Yet there I was.

And what stopped me from topping myself was that I was thinking about hell.

Imagine after I died, I woke up in hell.

Imagine if it was all real. Imagine that everything you'd heard about was real. Fire. Demons. People suffering. All of that. Forever. And it's waiting for you. It's just behind the curtain. It's right there.

I had a feeling, there in the toilet, of something unseen. It was like an invisible person was watching me, from inches away, almost nose to nose. I didn't feel like there was somebody there, but it was just that feeling of something unseen, waiting for me. And it scared me. Scared me enough to stop me from killing myself.

Fucking mental.

I truly do not believe in any of that stuff, I don't believe anything is waiting for me, waiting to get me. I know there isn't.

But if there is, well … it'll have to wait.

Twitter Trouble: Olympic Torch

The London 2012 Summer Olympics were about to happen. To celebrate, the Olympic torch was being passed all around the UK. There was some kind of rally happening. And I heard that it was going to be passing through Glasgow.

I asked on Twitter if that was true, and I asked who was going to be doing it. Was it somebody like Seb Coe, or some presenter off BBC Scotland, or what? I got told that it was going to be various people, some famous like James McAvoy, some not famous but regarded as local heroes or people that had done a lot of good.

I tweeted about it. I think I joked about how I was raging that I wasn't picked to carry the torch, being a local hero myself, hahaha. Then I heard that the torch was going to be carried up Byres Road, which wasn't far from where I stayed. So I made a snide wee tweet about that.

I said something like, 'Here, we should all go down to Byres Road and lock arms and not let them past.'

I was just joking, obviously.

I think I was saying it in the context of it being a protest of local hero Limmy not getting to carry the torch. Or maybe I was saying it just out of badness, the way you want to ruin everybody's happiness because you're not too happy yourself, like when you kick down a sandcastle. But I was just joking.

Not long after tweeting it, maybe that same day, the doorbell goes.

Lynn went to answer it, then she came walking in to the living room, and said the words you don't want to hear.

'The police are at the door. They want to speak to you.'

I was like, 'To me?'

I got up and walked to the door, trying to imagine what I'd done wrong. And I think I had that tweet down as one of the options.

I answered the door, and the police were wearing suits. They were the CID or something. I said, 'Alright?'

One of them said they were Detective something something, and this is Detective something. Could they come in and speak to me? I said aye, and led them into the living room. Lynn stayed in the kitchen.

They sat down and said that they'd been notified of a message I sent on social media. Something where I was encouraging people to disrupt the procession of the Olympic torch. And they wanted to know what that was about.

I was like, 'Oh right, that. Sorry, it was just a joke. No, I wasn't serious or anything, I'm not a protester or something. No, I come out with rubbish like that all the time.'

I was wondering who could have grassed me in.

One of the detectives said, 'Well, we've got to take all these seriously and follow them up. Because somebody might decide to do what you're suggesting.'

I said, 'Oh, no, I don't think anybody would, honest. People know that I'm joking. Are you familiar with Twitter? D'you know how it works, followers and all that?'

They said they weren't that familiar with it, and they looked a bit embarrassed to admit it. It was a fucking relief to see them slightly on the back foot, because I wasn't sure if I was getting handcuffed or something.

I said that I was a comedian type of person and the people who see my tweets are mostly people who are familiar with my sense of humour. But I understood that the tweets could reach easily influenced people, and that I'd delete the tweet right away, and I wouldn't joke about stuff like that again.

They were happy to hear that. They sort of apologised for having to visit me, and I said I was sorry for wasting their time, because they've got better things to do. Sorry, sorry, sorry.

They went away, and Lynn told me I was a stupid idiot.

And it was a stupid thing to do.

I really had to sort myself out. Whenever I get down or bored or stressed or whatever, I get these urges to say and do bad things, for a buzz. I want to do it even when

I'm not down, for a laugh. But I had to stop doing it. I wasn't just some guy any more, I wasn't just some cunt off the street, I wasn't a teenager or an anonymous steamer any more. I'd been on the telly, on the BBC, and I was in the process of making the third series of *Limmy's Show*. And there's me with the fucking polis at the door.

Breakdown

In 2013, when I was 38, I had what you would maybe call a breakdown. My mind just chucked in the towel.

At the end of 2012, when my third and final series of *Limmy's Show* was on the telly, me and Lynn moved out of our flat in Partick. It took about four months to move in to our new place, during which time we had to stay at Lynn's mum and dad's near Cumbernauld. That's when I started to crack up.

There were all these difficulties with trying to get the new house, all this shite that Lynn had to sort out by herself because I was clueless. She's since told me that that period was the closest she herself came to a meltdown, and she just never seems to have trouble with her mental health. She was at the end of her tether with me, I was doing fuck all to help. She was going mental and I was going mental. I was waking up every morning in that house with the knowledge that I was going to be a useless cunt that day. I could have at least done something nice for Lynn if I was useless with the practical stuff, but it didn't even cross my mind. I'm probably a naturally selfish person, but I sometimes go in even more of a bubble when I'm criticised for it. I clam up.

I was suicidal. It was Daniel's second birthday while we were staying there, and I'd had a meltdown the night before. Lynn asked me to get wrapping paper from the loft, and I asked a few stupid questions that caused an argument. I started stuttering. I was losing it. And I said that I couldn't do it any more. I got in a taxi and left, the night before my son's second birthday. I can't remember if I came back that same night or if I stayed in the empty Partick flat overnight, but either I wasn't there for his party or I was prepared to not be there.

I told Lynn at some point that I was thinking of topping myself, and she said, 'I don't want to hear it.' It had got that bad. She was fucking sick of my selfishness and her having to do everything. A horrible time.

When we eventually moved into the new house, the place was a mess and it took lots of renovation work, lots of phone calls to tradesmen and organising everything, which Lynn had to do all by herself. I just cannot pick up a phone and speak to one of these folk and know what the fuck I'm talking about. If Lynn was to ask me to phone an electrician and organise him updating the electrics or whatever it is, how would I do that? What do I want? Where do I want the sockets? Now that I'm typing it, it seems straightforward, but that's not how I think at the time. It's a fucking blur of confusion and anxiety.

There were more arguments, more things to be done. I woke up every morning and let out this big sigh. Every morning, this big sigh, like it was already the end of the day and I was knackered.

I was stripping the wallpaper, this hard-as-fuck type to remove, and I was stopping every now and then to just do nothing. To just stand there on the ladder with my mind blank.

Then Lynn wanted me to dig up this bush in the back garden. I was having trouble getting it out, so I started sawing it. But I barely had the strength to lift the saw. I was breaking down emotionally in a way that was making me physically weak. I'd never felt anything like it before. I'd seen people talk about it, about being so weak that they can't get off the couch, and I thought it was an exaggeration, but here it was.

I went into this downstairs toilet, which was more of a cupboard, and I shut the door and started crying. Just started crying in the dark. And I never cry. It wasn't just my eyes getting watery, it was full-blown crying, the face contorting and me making sounds like I was laughing.

I got out the cupboard and sat in the living room, and looked at a picture of my son as a baby. I started crying again, because I knew I had to kill myself. I just couldn't do this any more. I just couldn't.

I know it doesn't make sense, it doesn't make sense when I type it right now. Was I suicidal because stripping the wallpaper was a bit of a cunt? No, it was more than that. It was a combination of thoughts and feelings I'd had for weeks and months and years. I'm not good enough; I'm selfish and I can't seem to help it; I don't find day-to-day life enjoyable; I don't see this getting better, this is just the way I am and the way things are; I'm not a caring and loving dad, a caring and loving boyfriend, and I don't even care about or love myself. I'm sorry, but it's just too hard. It's pathetic, but it's just too hard.

I was crying looking at my son's picture, thinking about what my suicide note would say. He'd grow up and want to know how I could look at this picture of him as a baby, or look at him walking about, this two-year-old toddler, and for that not to be enough to stop me from killing myself.

I went to the doctor.

I had a pal whose husband had been taking antidepressants, one called citalopram, and she said he'd perked right up. I knew him well, I remember meeting him, and he didn't seem like a zombie. He seemed fine. I remembered her telling me that, and I'd been thinking about it. I didn't want to take mind-altering drugs, I wanted to be me. But I just thought, 'Go. Go to the doctor.'

So I went. And I was scared. There's something scary about talking about a problem with your mind or emotions, rather than a broken bone. It's debatable. And it's personal. It's about you as a person, not about a cut or a rash. It's nothing you can see. And you don't know exactly what to say. You don't know if they'll believe you.

I said, 'I've been not feeling well, mentally. I've been, em, suicidal. Been getting quite suicidal.' And I left it to him to say the next thing.

He said it was good that I'd come, and that 'the darkest hour is just before the dawn'.

I thought that was a bit out of character for a doctor, to be hitting out with some inspirational quote.

But then he gave me the contact details for some mental health people, and he offered me antidepressants, one of which was citalopram. I didn't think it was right that he was offering pills so quickly without having more information, but I took the prescription to the chemist and I got them anyway.

I told Lynn about them, and she said she hoped they worked. I told her that they took about a month or so to work, and I might get worse before I get better. I took one of the pills that day, then went to bed that night.

I woke up the very next morning a changed man.

I am not exaggerating.

I'd been waking up every morning with this big deflated sigh, this feeling of doom. But that morning I woke up feeling fit as a fiddle. I thought that it had to be my imagination, it had to be the placebo effect, because it said they took weeks to kick in. But I felt better than I'd felt for fucking ages.

As the weeks went on, I felt the pills take more of an effect. I didn't feel down. I didn't feel pessimistic. I felt happy. And I didn't feel unnaturally happy. I didn't feel like I'd be smiling and laughing at a funeral or anything. I just felt happy to be here. Happy to be alive.

It was the happiest I had ever been in my life.

The negative thoughts I'd always had, the ones that went round and round and wouldn't go away, they were gone. All the negative feelings, like regret and rumination and vengeance and anger and self-doubt and self-loathing and worrying about the future, all these feelings that would usually go around and around … I just forgot about them. I literally forgot. They'd pop into my mind for a second, then I'd forget why I cared. I was too busy just enjoying my life.

Lynn noticed the change. She said it was like a new, happier me, the same person but not so fucking down all the time. Lynn used to ask me if I wanted to go to this place or that, and I used to be like, 'Emmmm …

Hmmm, if you want.' Now I was always saying aye. Because I knew I'd be happy wherever I went.

I've read tweets from people on antidepressants saying that it's a misconception that the pills make you 'happy'. They just make you normal. But whatever you want to call it, I felt happy. And I did feel normal. I thought, 'Is this what everybody else has been feeling this whole time?'

There were side-effects, though. My mouth was dry, my face was red, I sometimes stuttered (more than usual), my short-term memory was fucked and it took ages to cum. I timed how long it took me to have a wank. It normally takes me about five minutes. The quickest I could have one on citalopram was 18 minutes.

A side-effect that I was expecting was that my creativity would be hampered, because I wouldn't have enough ambition or pain or desire or whatever drives me to make things. But that didn't happen. I wrote my *Limmy's Show Christmas Special* while on them. And I got into making Vines around that time. I made hundreds of them. If anything, the pills made me less precious about what I made. I didn't think about the downsides, I just went for it.

I absolutely loved citalopram. It's not for everybody, but it worked a treat for me.

But then it started to not work, from time to time. There would be periods of a few weeks when the pills seemed to not work, and I'd notice me getting into arguments with Lynn more. Instead of letting things go, I'd latch on to them and get defensive. Lynn noticed it, and I wondered what was going wrong. But then the pills would start working again, and I was back to 'normal'.

A few months later it happened again, so I started meditating to try and clear my mind of negative, repetitive thoughts. And it worked. (I'll tell you how I meditate in the next chapter.) Eventually the pills took over again. But then they stopped working again. And that's when I decided to chuck them.

I decided to chuck them because I wanted to feel a bit more consistent, rather than the pills working and not working. And I felt I'd sorted my head out enough. The meditating was working, I was eating healthily, I was exercising more. I think I'd sorted myself out. So I told Lynn I was going to come off them, and she told me I was stupid to do that. Why would I chuck these pills that had made me happy?

I decided to come off them, and not tell her.

I wouldn't tell the doctor either. You were supposed to come off them over a period of weeks or months, but I wanted to come off them quickly, whatever the consequences.

I felt that it was my decision. I worked out that one of the main problems with my mental health during all this time, for most of my life, was a lack of assertiveness.

It was a lack of self-confidence. I was always checking with other people to see if I was doing alright. I was always wanting to be like them or be liked by them or be approved by them or something like that. Maybe it went all the way back to my childhood. Maybe I've got some sort of learning difficulty or coping difficulty that made me rely too much on other people, made me want to check with them to see if I was doing alright, because I'm not a very good judge myself. But then I took it too far, and got into some bad habits. Whatever the reason, it was important now that I just did what I wanted, come what may.

I cut my dosage by half for three days, then down to a quarter for three days, then I chucked the pills in the bin. Doing it like that is supposed to be quite dangerous, but I didn't give a fuck. I'd been through all sorts with booze and drugs, this would be fuck all.

It took a week or so, but I started to feel sick. I started to feel seasick. I started to feel like I'd been on a roundabout or on swings for an hour, and my head was spinning. Just moving my eyes from side to side made me feel like I'd been spinning on the spot for ten minutes. A sickening, dizzy feeling. But I never told Lynn. We went to a swing park with Daniel when I was feeling like that, and I went on actual swings and a roundabout. I felt car sick as fuck, but when Lynn asked why I didn't look well I said it was because of the swings.

The sick feeling went away after a while, but I noticed my old ways come back. I was in the shower, and I noticed I was no longer happy. I was back to this cold and empty feeling. It wasn't sadness, it was just nothing. It was boredom, and I noticed my mind starting to think. My mind felt like a machine starting to power up again, needing things to think about to occupy the void. I would start trying to work out things that don't need to be worked out, like how to make showers better, or I'd wonder how soap works and I'd try to remember what the teacher said in chemistry.

Thinking, thinking, thinking.

I noticed my first negative thought when I was cycling through the toon. I saw a group of young guys across the road walk by a homeless woman, and they laughed at her. It made me angry, and I wanted to go over and ask them what they said, which I never would. I cycled on, and thought about those guys again, the cunts. Then I cycled more, and then I thought about those guys again, and what I could have said. Then I cycled more, and I thought about those guys again.

I hadn't thought that way during the whole time of me being on the pills. The pills just made me let go of things, which was good for my mental health, but perhaps bad for society, who knows. But these weren't thoughts that I would act on to make the world a better place, they just went round and around and around.

I kept on top of that by continuing to meditate. I'd do it every morning, whether I felt bad or good, and it worked. And I'd do it sometimes during the day. I'd do it in a café, or just sitting in the house. I'd try to remember how I felt on the pills, and I'd try to be like that. I'd just try to be happy, happy to just be here.

I felt like I'd really fucking cured myself. I'd always have to keep an eye on myself, but I felt so much better than I did before the pills. The pills helped me straighten my head out enough to straighten it out even further.

No more suicidal thoughts. Not for anything. Not for anybody. If it's a choice between killing me or killing you, I'd kill you.

I felt good.

How I Meditate

Before I went on antidepressants and I was tweeting about how bad I was feeling, people would say I should try meditating, and I thought they were fucking clowns. But after I came off the pills it's what helped keep me stable, it's what helped me clear my mind of repetitive, negative thoughts. Meditating is a way to clear my mind of all the shite, and it helps me keep bad thoughts away even when I'm not meditating.

There's nothing spiritual in it, for me. It's purely about controlling my mind. Here's how I do it. It's quite simple, but it can also be quite hard, depending on how you feel.

I sit somewhere where I'm sure I won't be disturbed. I just sit on a seat. I don't sit on the ground with my legs crossed or anything like that. But I try to be comfortable, whatever's best for my back.

I close my eyes, and all I try to do for the next ten or fifteen minutes is think about my breathing.

Nothing more.

That's it.

I don't try to control my breathing, I don't try to breathe all slowly, I don't count in my head or listen to music. I just think about it. I just feel it as it happens all by itself. In, and out. In, and out. I might think about the sound of the breathing through my nose, or the feeling in my chest, but all I try to think about is my breathing.

When another thought pops into my mind, about something I'm working on or a person or a song, I try to think about my breathing more. It's hard to not think of something once it's in your head. I don't try to block it out, I just think of the breathing more. It's a bit like listening to somebody talking to you at a party or a pub. You can hear all these other voices all around, there's nothing you can do about it, but by concentrating on that one voice you drown out all the others.

These annoying thoughts keep coming back while I'm meditating, but I keep thinking about my breathing. Sometimes I feel myself breathe out and not breathe in again for ages, like there was a tension that I wasn't aware of. I don't try to control it, I just let it do its thing.

I just think about the breathing. That's it.

And eventually, when I do it long enough, I get this feeling.

It's a feeling of the other thoughts and sounds in my head just switching off. It's like when a sound switches off that you weren't even aware of. And I'm left with this feeling of it just being me.

I'm not thinking about the past or the future, I'm not making plans or working anything out. I'm just being there and then, being all peaceful within myself. When it goes well, it makes me smile. Other times, I just enjoy it.

A stray thought might pop into my head, but I just get back to thinking about my breathing more.

And I keep doing it for however long I want. Maybe five minutes. Maybe I just stop right away once the thoughts have cleared. Maybe I sit for a good while.

Then I slowly open my eyes and feel refreshed. Things feel different. My mind feels a bit more in control. There's a comfort in knowing that I've caused my mind to change, that I've made myself feel a lot better, all by myself. I didn't stuff my face full of chocolate or check Twitter every two seconds or play some game that ends up doing my nut in. I did it all in my head.

If I do that every morning, there's a good chance of me having a good day. There's more chance of it working if I do it every day, because I'm better practised at it, so there's less pressure and I'm less upset if it doesn't work.

And the good thing about being well practised in shoving things out my mind is that I can do it during the day when I'm not meditating. If an annoying thought pops into my mind, a negative or bitter or vengeful or irritating thought, I can switch to a better thought to drown out the bad one. If the bad one keeps coming back, I keep thinking about the better one, until my mind gets the message.

So that's how I meditate, and I advise you to try it, if you haven't already. Everybody's mind is different, and it will definitely feel hard to begin with. But I guarantee you that if you get it to work even just once, that memory of it working will encourage you to come back and do it again.

Mind you, there's me saying that, but I haven't done it for a while. Not regularly, anyway.

Then again, my mind is currently in tatters. So that proves my point.

I'm going to meditate right now, and I'll let you know how I get on …

...

Right, I just did it. After 24 minutes I still couldn't get quite into it. I was almost falling asleep, because I was up late last night. It felt good and everything, but you want to try and stay awake.

Look, I've made a cunt of this chapter.

But honestly, try it.

My Last Sitcom

I was feeling better. I had another bash at writing a sitcom, but it didn't wind me up as much as doing the first one. I had two bashes, in fact, two sitcoms, and both of them got knocked back. Yet still, I was alright.

The first one was a sitcom that I called 'Family', where I played all four characters of this family in a house: the mum, dad and the two brothers. It was ambitious, technically, but I was sure I could pull it off without it being a nightmare.

The mum was based on the woman I played in the stripper sketch from the third series of *Limmy's Show*, where I shout 'Margaret! Margaret! Put it in your mouth!' A nasty piece of work, who has pit her sons against each other their whole life, resulting in them turning out very different from each other. One is a jailbird and a constant disappointment, but he's got ambitions to be a successful businessman like his brother; the other is privately having a breakdown, and secretly wishes he had the simple life of the other. The mum's got her own rivalries with her neighbours, and the dad's in the middle of it all as the voice of sanity.

I gave the idea to Channel 4, and they said they liked it. I wrote the script, and they liked that, but wanted a few tweaks. I did a few tweaks, and they liked it more. It was looking good, looking good. It was looking very good.

And then the commissioner moves to the BBC. And this new one takes his place, and says that she doesn't like it. The end.

The second shot at a sitcom was Falconhoof.

I'd considered doing a *Limmy's Show* spinoff before, but it felt like a step back to go and use an old character. It was almost too easy. But that was two sitcoms I'd got knocked back, and I wanted to make something. I wanted to make something because I'd enjoy it, plus I had this fucking mortgage to pay. So I pitched the idea for the pilot to the commissioner at BBC Scotland, and he said alright, I should write a script and he'll see what he thinks.

I wanted to make something a bit like a cross between *Curb Your Enthusiasm* and *The Larry Sanders Show*. In *Limmy's Show* the guy playing Falconhoof was obviously trying his best to make it work, but it always went tits up in some way. I wanted it to be the same with the rest of his life, partly due to him playing this Falconhoof guy on the telly.

In the pilot, *Adventure Call* has been under fire in the papers because weans have been phoning up, costing their parents a fortune. Falconhoof is in the papers, with a Photoshop job done of him leading weans like the Pied Piper of Hamelin, with all this money falling out their pockets. The guy who plays Falconhoof is worried, because he's a decent guy, but his boss doesn't give a fuck because the business gets all the money from the phone calls yet it'll never have to pay out any prize money because the weans aren't old enough. A series of events follows where Falconhoof tries to rehabilitate his image, including doing a fundraiser for a youth centre. After leaving the fundraiser, which was a success, some youngsters round the back of the centre ask him over for a picture. While he's there with them alone they involve him in some gambling; they insist, as a way for them to symbolically win their money back for all the weans that Falconhoof has stolen from. He gets hustled and cheated out of a small fortune to begin with, but then he manages to win all his money back in one go. He fucking jumps for joy at all the money in his hands.

Which, of course, is all caught on camera by onlookers.

I typed up the script. There's some more stuff in it, relationships, rivalries, the troubles with fame that are partly based on myself. I liked the script – it was more mainstream than the other two sitcoms, it was less experimental, and you already knew what the character was going to look and sound like. I didn't think it was a dead cert, but I was quite confident it would be a yes, pending some tweaks.

But it was a knock-back.

The commissioner said that it was too 'wordy' or 'talky', I think, and that he preferred my sketch stuff.

So that was that.

I thought if I can't get a sitcom with a character that's already made and liked by fans, if I can't get it commissioned by the same guy that commissioned *Limmy's Show*, then I can't get any sitcom with anycunt.

I didn't know what I was going to do. I got a bit more telly work, I did some stuff for *Charlie Brooker's Weekly Wipe*, and I did a couple of things for the iPlayer and for Sky. But other than that, there was nothing regular, nothing big. I didn't want to go back and do *Limmy's Show*, I didn't want to bleed it dry. And I didn't want to go back to live stuff. That also felt like a step back, plus I'd been away from it for so long that it gave me a nervy feeling just thinking about it again.

I really didn't know what to do. But like I said to you earlier in the book, I'm such a lucky, lucky bastard sometimes.

Books

It was mid-2014, when I was 39. I was starting to worry a bit about what work I had coming up. I was thinking, 'What will you be up to in two years from now? Because it doesn't look like much. It almost looks like this is you on the decline. You're not in the gutter yet, you're safe for now, because *Limmy's Show* took care of that. But now *Limmy's Show* is gone. Seriously, where will you be in two or three years' time? Who knows, you might actually have to get yourself a *real job*.'

Around that time I'd been writing wee stories on Twitter and Facebook, out of boredom. Just to entertain myself. I'd type something up in half an hour or something, something daft, and I'd see the reaction. I loved writing them.

A publisher saw the stories, and got in touch with my agent to ask if I wanted to write a book.

Too right.

Too fucking right I did.

How fucking lucky was that?

He suggested something like *The World According to Limmy*, a mix of thoughts and stories and autobiographical things, but I just fancied doing the stories. He said that was fine, thank fuck.

It didn't take me long to think of the title: *Daft Wee Stories*. It explained what the book was about, but it was also a bit of a defence mechanism. It's like the title said: 'Don't get your hopes up. And don't criticise it. They're just daft wee stories.'

The book was to be 70,000 words, and I was given about six months to write it, till the end of the year. That sounded fine. I read Stephen King saying that he does 2,000 words a day, which is 10,000 a week, which is about 40,000 a month, and 80,000 in two months. 2,000 words a day sounded fine, and I had six months. It's the same way I wrote this book right here.

So I just sat in the house, or went out to cafés, and I wrote 2,000 words worth of stories every day. I'd either make something up on the spot, based on something I saw in the café, or it would be from an idea I took a note of elsewhere.

For example, I was sitting in a café, and I thought, 'You've got to get an idea from something you see in here.' I looked about, and I saw Russian dolls on a shelf. And I got the idea of a person like that, a person with a person inside them, then a person inside that, and on and on and on. I imagined this lassie, called Sally, who feels a bit ill one day, a bit sluggish, and she gets rushed to hospital. They cut her open, and there inside is another one of her, slightly smaller. She decides to name herself Sally 2. She lives a normal life for a few weeks, but then she feels sluggish and heavy as well. They cut her open, and out comes Sally 3. And so it goes on, until she's a foot tall, then as small as an atom.

Then even smaller than that. A size so small you can't get your head around. A size smaller than time and space and imagination.

And see that size? See that size, that unimaginable size?

That's yer da's cock.

I didn't know how else to end the story, so I ended with that. It was a childish way to end a 1,200-word story, but it made me burst out laughing in the café when I typed it. So that was that. I imagined it getting a good reaction when I read it out on the book tour, or getting a groan.

That was another thing that was going to be happening. A book tour.

Not only did I have a book coming out, but I'd be doing a book tour in mid-2015 when the book was out, my first live thing since the Fringe in 2008. I was looking forward to it. I hadn't fancied doing live stuff all those years, I didn't want to go back to the unpredictability of it all and the worries that came with it. But this would be different. I'd be reading from a book. Then I'd be doing a Q&A, and I can talk like fuck. Remember I said that people would come up to me in the street to say hello, then I'd talk so much that they had to make their excuses and leave? Well, talking like fuck and answering questions would be no bother at all. It would be a fucking pleasure. And then, best of all, a book signing, where I'd get to meet everycunt, I'd get to shake the hands of people who liked my stuff, there would be smiling and happiness and patter and everything.

When the book was finished and printed, I got sent out an early copy. And what a feeling to see your stories printed in a book. An actual book that you can smell.

I picked out what stories I would read for the tour, ones with a bit of a punchline, and I thought up some patter to say to the audience. But before I did the tour I wanted to get a taste of being in front of an audience again, just in case – a bit like when I did that first bit of stand-up, to prepare me. So I went on Richard Herring's podcast, which was filmed in front of a few hundred people at the Leicester Square Theatre. I read 'The Size of Sally' at the end of the interview (that's what I called that Sally story), to see what they thought of it. At the end, I pointed to somebody in the audience to say, 'That's your da's cock,' and everybody burst out laughing.

Thank fuck, man. Thank fuck.

I did the book tour up and down Britain, and I loved it. I loved sitting on trains and staying in hotels, then doing each show, then the signings afterwards where I met everybody and got pictures with them, with people saying nice things and me saying nice things to them. I just fucking loved it.

Sometimes when things are going well for me I don't appreciate it at the time. I worry too much, or I take it for granted. It's only later, when things aren't as good, or when the worry is no longer an issue, that I look back and think, 'Christ, that was a good time, that. I wish I could go back and enjoy it more.' But I remember being aware of how much I was enjoying it while it was happening. I remember thinking, 'This isn't a rose-tinted memory. I'm enjoying this right here and fucking now. This is the life.'

Because of the book tour, I decided to do a kind of live *Limmy's Show* tour as well, called 'Limmy Live'. I reckoned that if I was going to be getting into live stuff with the book tour, I may as well go all in. That sold out all four nights at the 3,000-seater Armadillo in Glasgow, and I was so fucking happy to be filled with confidence again. I walked about the audience shouting, 'She's turned the weans against us!' in just a pair of pants, with a fake cock flopping out the front, and a big brown stain on my arse like I've shat myself. There are videos on YouTube – it was a fucking highlight of my entire life. (I also did a couple of shows down south in Manchester and London that didn't sell out, they didn't make any money, partly due to costs like it costing five grand for lights. Just for that London one, it cost five grand for lights. And that was just to fucking rent them. Can you fucking believe that? Look, I don't want to talk about it.)

After that, I went back to writing another book of short stories, called *That's Your Lot*. I wanted to write something a bit darker than *Daft Wee Stories*, a tiny wee bit more serious, with fewer punchlines, more in that slice-of-life style where you just get a glimpse into somebody's life, and then the story ends, that's your lot. Hence the title. Then I did a UK & Ireland tour of that, my first time being to Ireland.

Oh, that reminds me …

I got a wee surprise visitor from the old days. Remember I said that when I first did the Fringe people from my past would occasionally turn up? Well, guess who turned up at my *That's Your Lot* book tour, in Dublin of all places?

My evil presence!

I was just about to go on stage, in front of 900 people at this venue in Dublin called Vicar Street. I was looking forward to it, albeit with the usual slight nerves. I was told that I'd be going on in a few seconds, and I geared myself up for walking on. But then I got told that there would be a five-minute delay.

That fucked with my mind, for some reason. I think it was because I try to stay calm before going on. I try to keep the nerves under control by partially meditating and just thinking about something else, but when I know I'm just about to walk on I can let all of that go. I don't need to hold it together, and I can let the adrenaline kick in. Well, because I thought I was on in a few seconds, I let go, but when I found out I actually had another five minutes I found it hard to get back to that calm state. It wobbled me a bit. My defences were down. And that's when the evil presence turned up.

A voice in my head, one that didn't feel like my own, said, 'Oh, this isn't going well. This is going to be a bad one.'

I froze. Because I knew what that voice was.

When I tried to ignore it, it became more dominant. It became more mischievous. It said, 'It's me. I'm back. And I'm going to ruin this for you. Haha. I'm going to ruin this.'

I tried to fight it off. I might even have thought, 'Please, don't. Please.' I was getting scared.

But the voice said, 'Haha, listen to them all out there. I'm going to ruin this for you. I'm going to be in your head the whole time. When you're trying to read, I'm going to be here, and I'm going to do things. You won't be able to read. All you're doing is reading from a fucking book, and you won't even be able to do that.'

It felt fucking bad, because I knew it was possible. I imagined having to run off the stage.

But I told myself, 'Just think of the audience. It's not about you, it's about them. Don't think of yourself, think about them. Entertain them. Reach out to them. When you get out there, look them in the eyes, like you like to do. See a smiling face and smile back. I bet when you see that first smiling face, that'll be it, you'll be fine.'

So that's what I did. When I finally went on, I looked at some faces down the front row, different faces, people smiling, and that took me out of myself.

And it turned out to be the best night of that tour, no joke.

I fucking love the book tours and I'm looking forward to the tour for this.

I'm looking forward to you reading it and seeing what you think – if you like it, if you think it's funny or sad or mental or desperate or actually quite boring and goes on a bit too much about certain things and not enough about others, I don't know. It could be a dud, or it could be a career-ender.

That would be funny, if it was a career-ender. I've got some more telly stuff in the pipeline, maybe more of *Limmy's Homemade Show* on the BBC, but wouldn't it be funny if some of the bad stuff in this book threw a spanner in the works? Or what if this book fucked things up for me so badly that I became some sort of pariah and nobody came to my book tour? I don't think there's anything that bad in here, but you never know these days.

Well, it's printed now.

Fuck it.

Right Now

I'd like to end the book by letting you know what I'm up to right now.

Right now, I'm sitting at a desk in this wee home office we've got, finishing this book. I want it finished pronto, so that I can play some games. I've just bought myself a new computer and a mic and all these other things so that I can take my game streaming to the next level. I've been getting quite obsessed with it.

I got so obsessed with streaming games recently that me and Lynn nearly broke up. In fact, I think we actually did break up. She'd had enough, of me being up to all hours, neglecting her and Daniel. It wasn't just that, it was other things. But she'd had enough, and I was looking for a new flat and everything.

We decided not to do it, and I said I'd change, I'd try and stop all this. If it isn't booze, it's games. If it isn't games, then it's something else.

I made an appointment with the doctor because I was feeling suicidal again. I said to the doctor that I think I've got ADHD. I don't know if it's a real thing, but I looked it up and it basically describes me. So I got referred to some mental health person, who I'm meeting in a couple of weeks. If they say I've got ADHD, what then? Will it help? Can I force Lynn and Daniel to put up with my shite because I've got a condition? I'll probably look up some websites to give me advice, and maybe tweet about it. But other than that, how will a diagnosis help? I don't know. I'm just curious to know. I just want an explanation. But at the end of the day I don't really care, depending on how I feel.

I really don't want to lose Lynn, I really don't. I love her and I love Daniel and I don't want to have to move out and visit this house rather than live here. I've been trying to make an effort. I asked her to show me how to make me a couple of meals, so that I could make dinner for a change. It's a pathetic attempt, really. I kept it up for a few weeks, but I'm starting to slip, I can feel it. And I've started staying up all night playing games again. Not as late as before, but late.

Help me.

No, I'm really going to try and screw the nut.

It was my 44th birthday two days ago, on the 20th of October. I stayed up late, streaming games. That then made me knackered the next day, which was yesterday, so I fell asleep a bit early, about 9.30 p.m. Then I woke up at 12.30 a.m. and I couldn't get back to sleep. I was thinking of finishing this book. So I just got up and started typing. I haven't been to sleep yet, and it's almost midday. I feel a bit away with it. But it's hopefully a one-off.

When I've finished the book I'll move on to planning for the book tour, what I'm going to say and do in front of the audience. Then I'll be writing some telly stuff. But you know what I'd rather be doing than the telly stuff? Streaming games. How fucking spoiled is that?

I really don't want to fuck things up. I don't want to break up with my family.

I was lying next to Daniel the other day in bed, while he was playing some Lego game on the PS4. He was talking away to me while he was playing, while I was under the covers with my arm around him. I was listening to his wee voice and the wee sounds he makes, while I was all cuddled up with him, this wee warm eight-year-old body lying next to me. It was just wonderful. And I was thinking to myself, this feels like lying in the sunshine. Not like on holiday when it's fucking roasting, I mean in Scotland where it's mostly cloudy and rainy and cold, but then you get this wee day or two of sunshine. And you tilt your face up towards it with your eyes closed. It feels good on your skin, it feels good on the outside and good on the inside, it just puts you in a right good mood.

It was like that.

And I told him. I told him, because I want to make sure he knows how I feel.

Fucking hell, this sounds like a suicide note, haha. Sorry.

I'm fine. I don't want to end on a downer.

I just want a laugh.

That's all I fucking want. That's all I've ever wanted, really. That's what I want now, that's what I want forever and ever.

I just want a laugh.